the food of **Indonesia**

Delicious Recipes from Bali, Java and the Spice Islands

by **Heinz von Holzen & Lother Arsana**
photos by **Heinz von Holzen**
introduction by **Wendy Hutton**

TUTTLE Publishing

Tokyo | Rutland, Vermont | Singapore

Published by Tuttle Publishing, an imprint of Periplus Editions (HK) Ltd
www.tuttlepublishing.com

ISBN 978-0-8048-4513-7 pb
Previously published as *Authentic Recipes from Indonesia*
ISBN 978-0-7946-0320-5 hc

Distributed by

North America, Latin America & Europe
Tuttle Publishing
364 Innovation Drive
North Clarendon, VT 05759-9436 U.S.A
Tel: 1 (802) 773-8930; Fax: 1 (802) 773-6993
info@tuttlepublishing.com
www.tuttlepublishing.com

Japan
Tuttle Publishing
Yaekari Building, 3rd Floor
5-4-12 Osaki, Shinagawa-ku, Tokyo 141-0032
Tel: (81) 3 5437-0171; Fax: (81) 3 5437-0755
sales@tuttle.co.jp
www.tuttle.co.jp

Asia Pacific
Berkeley Books Pte. Ltd.
3 Kallang Sector #04-01, Singapore 349278
Tel: (65) 6741-2178
Fax: (65) 6741-2179
inquiries@periplus.com.sg
www.tuttlepublishing.com

Indonesia
PT Java Books Indonesia
Kawasan Industri Pulogadung
Jl. Rawa Gelam IV No. 9, Jakarta 13930
Tel: (62) 21 4682-1088; Fax: (62) 21 461-0206
crm@periplus.co.id
www.periplus.com

All recipes were tested in the Periplus Test Kitchen.
Photo credits: All photos by Heinz von Helzen
except page 6 by Kal Muller, pages 7, 8, 9, 10 and 14 by Jill Gocher.

Acknowledgments: The authors and publisher wish to thank Peter
Settler, Regional Manager of Hyatt Indonesia for his support and
enthusiasm. A special *terima kasih* to Marcel Isaak and his team
for the food preparation. Nyoman Wijana and I. Made Cornelius
of the Balai Pendidikan dan Latihan Parawisata at Nusa Dua, Bali,
provided invaluable assistance and access to their archive of recipes. Puri Sakan Antiques Art Gallery, Njana Tilem Gallery, Arts of
Asia Gallery, Architectural Ceramics and Jenggala Keramik kindly
provided woodcarvings, antiques, *objets d'art*, textiles and ceramics
for photography.

25 24 23   10 9 8 7 6 5
Printed in China   2309EP

"Books to Span the East and West"

Tuttle Publishing was founded in 1832 in the small New
England town of Rutland, Vermont [USA]. Our core values
remain as strong today as they were then—to publish
best-in-class books which bring people together one
page at a time. In 1948, we established a publishing
outpost in Japan—and Tuttle is now a leader in publishing
English-language books about the arts, languages and
cultures of Asia. The world has become a much smaller
place today and Asia's economic and cultural influence
has grown. Yet the need for meaningful dialogue and
information about this diverse region has never been
greater. Over the past seven decades, Tuttle has
published thousands of books on subjects ranging from
martial arts and paper crafts to language learning and
literature—and our talented authors, illustrators, designers
and photographers have won many prestigious awards.
We welcome you to explore the wealth of information
available on Asia at **www.tuttlepublishing.com.**

Contents

Food in Indonesia
A Cuisine as Exciting and Diverse as the Country Itself

Indonesia is the world's largest archipelago—thousands of tropical islands ranging from some of the world's largest to mere tiny coral atolls marooned in a sapphire sea. With snow-capped mountains and lush rainforests, arid savannahs and irrigated rice fields, it's hard to imagine a more appropriate national motto for this nation than *Bhinneka Tunggal Ika*—Unity in Diversity.

Over the past two thousand years, powerful Buddhist, Hindu and Muslim kingdoms rose and fell in Sumatra, Java and Borneo, attracting merchants from as far away as China, the Middle East and India, as well as nearby Siam and Malacca. Some of the archipelago's tiny eastern isles were the original Spice Islands—the only places in the world where clove and nutmeg trees grew, and a powerful magnet for traders and pirates.

European explorers and merchants were not far behind. Portuguese, Spanish, English and Dutch ships set forth on voyages of discovery to these islands during the 16th and 17th centuries. The Dutch were the final victors in the battle for control over the region, introducing a plantation system to the main islands, where laborers toiled to produce sugar, spices, rubber, tea and coffee (the original "cup of Java"). A nationalist movement arose as early as 1908, but it was not until 1949 that the Republic of Indonesia came into being, after an armed struggle against the Dutch following Indonesia's declaration of independence in 1945.

With its enormous geographic and cultural diversity, it is not surprising that the food of Indonesia is tremendously varied also. However, as restaurants in Indonesia tend to focus on the dishes served only in Java and Sumatra, many non-Indonesians are unaware that each region actually has its own distinct cuisine. These indigenous regional styles have been influenced to varying degrees over the centuries by ingredients and cooking styles from China, India, Europe and other parts of Asia.

A "typical" Indonesian meal might be described as a simple mound of rice accompanied by several savory side dishes of vegetable, fish or perhaps a meat or poultry dish, with a chili-hot condiment or sambal on the side and peanuts, crispy wafers (*krupuk*) and fried shallots sprinkled on top to provide a crunchy contrast. While such a description might be valid for much of Java, Sumatra and Bali, in other areas of the archipelago, the staple might be sago, cassava, yams or corn instead of rice.

Increasing numbers of visitors are discovering the rich cultural diversity of Indonesia, venturing off the beaten Bali-Java-Sumatra tourist track. Let us take you on a voyage of culinary discovery, exploring the unknown and revealing more about the already familiar.

Eating your way across the archipelago

What do a feast of pig steamed over hot stones in an earth oven, a ritual *selamatan* centered upon a golden rice mountain blessed by Muslim prayers, a bamboo tube of buffalo meat spiked with chilies roasted over a fire, and satays of minced seafood mixed with spices and fresh coconut all have in common? They're just some of the foods I have enjoyed in travels throughout Indonesia over more than two decades. Visitors encountering the limited noodle and *nasi goreng* fare found in most Indonesian restaurants might be forgiven for thinking that there's more unity than diversity in the food here. It's only if you brave the local *warung* or simple food stalls (as opposed to those run by migrants offering the ubiquitous *soto* or *mie bakso*), if you arrive when a festival is going on or, best of all, are able to stay in Indonesian homes, that you have a chance of discovering the diversity of Indonesia's native cuisines.

Some 3,200 feet (1,000 meters) up in the highlands of Irian Jaya, in western New Guinea, for example, lies a fertile, stream-slashed valley isolated from the world by almost impenetrable swamps and jungle-covered mountains. The Baliem Valley, discovered by explorers in 1938 and visited by the first anthropologists only in 1961, is the home of the Stone Age Dani people. They are skilled gardeners growing a variety of vegetables, yet 90 percent of their diet consists of various preparations of sweet potatoes. Although some 70 varieties are grown, after several days of eating this admirable tuber for breakfast, lunch and dinner, an outsider finds they all begin to taste alike.

While trekking in this beautiful valley in 1976, we passed a hamlet where great activity was taking place. Like all Indonesians, the Dani are extremely hospitable and literally dragged me and my two young children into a compound to join what proved to be a wedding feast. The men, splendid in penis gourds, faces painted with colored clay, and feathers stuck in their woolly black hair, lounged about playing bamboo mouth harps. The women, naked but for a string skirt perched precariously on their hips and almost knee-deep in freshly slaughtered pig, busily wrapped chunks of meat in leaves and stacked them onto river stones heated by a fire. Mounds of the inevitable sweet potatoes were laid on top of the pork, followed by a huge pile of leaves. The whole lot was then left to steam—just like a Maori *hangi* which, as a child, I had regarded as unique to New Zealand.

OPPOSITE: Rice is the basis of every main meal, with side dishes of meat, poultry, fish or vegetables plus crunchy garnishes and the ubiquitous fiery-hot sambals or chili sauces and relishes.

The food was eventually pronounced cooked and a leaf filled with pork was handed to me by an incredibly filthy woman. As I sat staring at the steaming pork, I thought of all the diseases I might catch. Sheer hunger and desperation for something other than sweet potato finally won out. Unwrapping my little packet of salt (a precious item in the valley, where it could be traded for other goods), I sprinkled some on the pork and took my first mouthful. Moist, sweet, full of flavor—I will never forget my Dani pig feast! Even the sweet potatoes tasted good steamed in this earth oven (and I suffered no ill after-effects whatsoever).

By contrast, the central Javanese city of Yogyakarta seems to be located on an entirely different planet. Ancient stone temples—including the famous Borobudur and the exquisite spires of Hindu Prambanan—rise up from the surrounding rice fields, while the classic cone of Mount Merapi periodically showers the land with rich volcanic ash.

The Javanese of Yogyakarta and nearby Surakarta are proud of their refined culture, their dances, *gamelan* music, *batik* fabric and intricate handicrafts. Theirs is a highly structured society in which harmony depends upon consideration for others and the group is more important than the individual. Ritual events are marked by a communal feast (*selamatan*), so it was appropriate that our arrival in the household of a Yogya family, where we were to stay for a year, was the occasion for such a feast.

Prayers were said to confer blessings upon our family and everyone present. The centerpiece of the *selamatan* is a cone-shaped mound of yellow rice, symbolic of the holy Hindu Mount Meru. (Although most Javanese are Muslim, earlier animistic, Buddhist and Hindu observances are still incorporated in their rituals.) At least a dozen dishes accompany the rice, including *gudeg* (young jackfruit stewed in palm sugar, coriander and coconut milk); fried chicken which is first simmered in spiced coconut milk; fermented soybean cakes (**tempeh**) fried with shrimp and sweetened with palm sugar; red chili sambal; and deep-fried crispy shrimp wafers (*krupuk*). The overall impression is one of subtlety and sweetness—a harmonious blend that is quintessentially Javanese.

At yet another end of the spectrum is the food of the west Sumatran region of Padang. If you like it hot and spicy (and thousands of Indonesians do, for Padang restaurants are found in most cities throughout the country), you'll have no hesitation in calling this the best cuisine of Indonesia. In a nation full of stunning scenery, the rugged mountains, lakes and glorious coastline of west Sumatra more than hold their own. The picturesque town of Bukittinggi ("High Hill"), the heartland of the Minang people, is perfect for sampling the local food.

This is one of the few cuisines best enjoyed in a restaurant or simple eating shop, since it is the spicy counterpart of a buffet. Portions of as many as 20 different dishes are carried from their display counter and placed on the table in front of you. You help yourself to whatever you want, paying only for what you eat. If you don't fancy the goat brains simmered in a rich, spicy coconut gravy, never mind, try the chicken in coconut with lemongrass, black slices of beef *dendeng*, large prawns coated with ground chili, or eggs in spicy sambal—the list literally goes on and on.

Most people describe Padang food as spicy, but dried spices are only one part of the story. In the market of Bukittinggi, where the proud Minang women are clothed in vivid purple velvet, there are mounds of cinnamon, pepper, coriander, chili powder, cumin and fennel—and also fresh chilies, ginger, garlic, shallots, galangal, turmeric, lemongrass, basil, fragrant lime and *salam* leaves and pungent dried shrimp paste. Nearby lie piles of ripe brown coconuts, their flesh grated to make the rich, creamy milk that soothes (if only slightly) the impact of the spices.

Endless islands, endless variety

With its thousands of miles of coastline, the orchid-shaped island of Sulawesi (Celebes) at the center of the archipelago is renowned for its freshly-caught fish. *Ikan bakar*, fish roasted over charcoal and served with a variety of dipping sauces, is a firm regional favorite, yet one of my most memorable meals in Sulawesi was in the highlands of Tana Toraja, where the villages lie marooned like islands in a vast sea of paddy fields.

Anxious to see the famous Torajan cliff burial sites with their wooden statues of the deceased, I spent almost an entire evening bumping by bus from Makasar to Rantepao. Awaking after a couple of hours' sleep, I noticed a stream of people on the road in front of my *losmen*. They were heading for a funeral, the most important event in the Torajan life cycle and an occasion for much ritual feasting.

Not long afterwards, I was seated in one of the bamboo shelters built to house guests during the lengthy funeral celebrations. Streams of men staggered up the slippery hillside bearing stout bamboo cups filled with frothing local palm wine (*tuak*), and with pigs strung by their feet from bamboo poles. The inevitable and somewhat gruesome slaughter of pigs and water buffalo was followed by the preparation of *piong*, bamboo tubes stuffed with chunks of lightly-salted meat, fresh blood, spinach leaves and a few fiery bird's-eye chilies. The bamboo tubes were stoppered with banana leaves and roasted over an open fire. Eaten with excellent hill rice and washed down with *tuak*, this was indeed a memorable feast.

Feasts are commonplace also in Bali, and I have spent many happy hours helping to chop and pound seasonings, slicing boiled pig's ear for the ceremonial *lawar* salads, coloring rice cakes and composing ritual village temple offerings. Even relatively simple food in Bali can be excellent. Other Indonesians may sniff that the Balinese extend their satays by adding coconut rather than using only meat or chicken, yet the local *sate lilit* made of highly seasoned

chopped seafood or poultry mixed with coconut and molded around stalks of fragrant lemongrass, is the best satay I've sampled in the entire archipelago.

The interior highlands of the so-called wilds of Borneo bring back wonderful memories of wild boar caught in the surrounding rainforest and smoked over a fire, of tender, sweet bamboo shoots thrusting up through the soil, and of wild ferns that rival baby asparagus for flavor.

Travel in Indonesia always means food, not just at the destination but en route, too. Buses stop at 2 am so that passengers can buy snacks from the villagers who sell, in the light of their flickering kerosene lamps, the delicacy for which they are renowned. Passengers on board ship share their home-prepared boneless stuffed fish or sticky rice rolls enclosing savory stuffings. Endless islands, endless variety, endless generosity. One could go on eating across Indonesia forever.

OPPOSITE: Dani tribesmen from the Baliem valley in Irian Jaya starting a fire to cook the inevitable meal of sweet potatoes. ABOVE: A plentiful supply of bamboo makes it a logical cooking utensil in Tana Toraja, Sulawesi. These Torajan men are preparing *piong*—bamboo tubes stuffed with meat—for a funeral feast.

Tropical Islands of Spice and Rice
An Archipelago of Snow-capped Mountains, Rainforest, Rice Fields, Swamps and Savannah

Stretching some 5,000 miles (8,000 kilometers) from the northwestern tip of Sumatra to the swamps of southeastern Irian Jaya, Indonesia's 18,000 or so islands (home to some 235 million people) extend from roughly 6 degrees north of the equator to 11 degrees south. The large islands of Sumatra, Java, Borneo (where three-quarters of the land mass is occupied by Indonesian Kalimantan) and Bali were part of the Asian mainland until they became permanently separated at the end of the last Ice Age.

Indonesia lies within the so-called "Ring of Fire," the meeting point of two of the earth's tectonic plates, which gives rise to frequent seismic activity. Smoldering volcanoes —like the Hindu god, Shiva, both Creator and Destroyer— periodically shower fertile ash over the land. Most of the western islands of Indonesia are lush and evergreen. While Borneo has rainforests and swampy coastlines, Java and Sumatra abound with fertile gardens, coconut groves and paddy fields. Fast-flowing rivers and glorious beaches complete the vision of a tropical paradise.

All of Indonesia enjoys tropical warmth and relatively high humidity, and most areas experience a dry season followed by life-giving monsoon rains. However, the eastern islands of the archipelago (especially Nusa Tenggara, the long chain of southeastern islands running from Lombok east to Timor) are rocky and semi-arid and the dry season here is longer and harsher, with the land often being degraded by tree-felling and subsequent erosion as a result.

Sulawesi (the Celebes), the strangely-shaped island at the center of Indonesia, has a variety of climates and different parts receive their monsoon rains at different times. Farther east, the Spice Islands of Maluku (the Moluccas) conform to the image of the lush tropics, while Irian Jaya (the western portion of New Guinea) has everything from swamps to rainforest to the highest mountain east of the Himalayas, the 16,000-foot (5,000-meter) snow-capped Mount Jaya.

The staple throughout Indonesia is rice, which is grown both in irrigated paddies (where up to three crops a year can be achieved by using special strains of rice and fertilizers) and in non-irrigated fields, which depend on the monsoon rains. In many areas of the archipelago, however, insufficient rainfall or unsuitable terrain make rice growing impossible, and crops such as sweet potato, tapioca (also known as cassava or manioc), corn and sago—a sticky starch scraped from the trunk of a palm tree—are the staples. Those who can afford it will buy rice imported from other regions of Indonesia, but in very remote areas, the traditional staple still reigns supreme. For economy, Indonesians sometimes add corn or sweet potato to their daily rice to give it extra substance; this also has the bonus of varying the flavor.

Not surprisingly for an archipelago, the most popular accompaniment to the staple food is fish, which is often simply fried with a little seasoning of sour tamarind, turmeric and salt, or simmered in seasoned water or coconut milk. There are, of course, hundreds of more complex recipes for both freshwater fish (often raised in ponds) as well as ocean fish. Because of limited transport and refrigeration, however, dried fish is more commonly encountered than fresh fish in many areas. Tiny dried whitebait known as *ikan teri* add flavor as well as protein to a number of savory snacks and spicy or crunchy sambals.

Although vegetables are grown throughout Indonesia, they do not figure prominently in the diet. Certain wild leaves and the young leaves of plants cultivated for their fruit or tubers (such as starfruit, papaya, sweet potatoes and tapioca) are cooked as vegetables. These are supplemented with a few easily grown vegetables, such as water spinach (*kangkung*), runner beans, eggplant, pumpkins and cucumbers. Elevated areas, especially in islands with rich volcanic soil, are perfect for temperate climate vegetables. The Dutch brought carrots, potatoes, cauliflower, cabbage and tomatoes, enthusiastically adopted by Indonesians.

OPPOSITE: Lush paddy fields, coconut palms and a distant volcano (in this case, Bali's Mount Agung) create the exquisite scenery typical of Bali, Java and Sumatra. ABOVE: Millions of acres of irrigated rice fields provide not only the staff of life but eels, small fish, food for the ducks and a pleasant place for cattle to cool down.

Indonesia's cuisines, especially in the major islands, have borrowed ingredients and cooking styles from many sources over the centuries. Arab and Indian traders brought their spices, sweet rose essence and one or two popular dishes (including Indian Martabak, a type of pancake found at thousands of food stalls).

The Spanish were responsible for the introduction of chilies, which they discovered in the New World and carried to the islands of the Philippines. These fiery fruits swept throughout Southeast Asia and India, and are so firmly established as part of the local cuisine that it's hard to imagine what the food was like here without them.

Despite their long period as colonial rulers, the Dutch, apart from the introduction of new vegetables and bread, did not have an enormous impact on the local cuisines. A word here about the so-called "Indonesian" *rijsttafel*. This was a colonial invention, a larger-than-life adaptation of the Indonesian style of serving rice with several savory side dishes and condiments. With time, money and plenty of servants to make almost anything possible, the Dutch developed a "rice table" where as many as 18–20 dishes might be served, each borne into the dining room by a comely maiden or uniformed "boy."

It is the Chinese who have had the greatest influence on Indonesian cooking. They introduced the ubiquitous noodles (*mie*); soy sauce, which the Indonesians modified to suit their taste by adding sugar (*kecap manis*); mung beans used to make bean sprouts (*taugeh*); tofu and soybeans, also used to make the excellent and nutritious tempeh.

Islands that changed the world

Apart from the crumbling remains of Portuguese and Dutch forts, there's little that sets several small Moluccan islands apart from countless other islands in Indonesia. Yet five of these islands were once the only place in the world where cloves grew, while another nearby group, the Bandas, were the sole source of nutmeg and mace. These islands were literally responsible for starting the Age of Exploration and for the discovery of the Americas by Christopher Columbus.

With today's refrigeration and food processing, it's hard to fully appreciate the importance of spices in earlier times. Cloves, pepper and nutmegs were sought by the Romans, Egyptians and Chinese as long as 2,000 years ago, used in cooking to add flavor and to help mask the flavors of less-than-fresh meat, to perfume the air during funerals and to sweeten the mouth. They were also used in medicines, magic potions and embalming recipes.

During the Middle Ages, the spice trade in Europe was controlled by Arab merchants, who purchased spices from Indian traders. They kept prices astronomically high by supplying Venetian merchants, who distributed the spices to the rest of Europe. The search for the source of these rare and expensive items—worth far more than gold or precious metal—caused Christopher Columbus to stumble upon the Americas (he thought he was going to reach Indonesia). Other voyages of exploration were made by the Portuguese, who eventually reached the Spice Islands of Indonesia at the beginning of the 16th century, followed by the Spanish, English and Dutch.

In 1602 the Dutch set up the East India Company to exploit the riches of the archipelago that was eventually to become Indonesia. They ruthlessly achieved a total monopoly in the spice trade and any grower who traded "illegally" was punished by having his clove trees cut down. In the 19th century, however, clove seedlings were smuggled out of the Spice Islands, ending the Dutch monopoly and eventually causing prices to come tumbling down.

Ironically, more cloves are now grown in northern Sulawesi and Zanzibar than in Maluku, and Indonesia now imports cloves to meet the demand for the spice. Don't expect to find it in many Indonesian dishes, however—most of the cloves literally go up in smoke, added to tobacco in the crackling *kretek* cigarettes.

Despite the drop in value of these spices (which could realize a profit of 1,000 percent for early explorers who returned with a full cargo), woven mats of drying cloves are still a common sight in Maluku. Picked green, the fragrant nail-shaped flower bud of the *Eugenia aromatica* tree is sundried for several days, turning beige until finally the familiar rich dark brown cloves found on supermarket shelves around the world appear. Tall nutmeg trees, regarded by many as the most beautiful of cultivated trees, still thrive on the islands of Banda and, to a lesser extent, on Ambon. The ripe fruit is picked and the hard fragrant nut extracted; often the nimble fingers of children are employed to separate the bright scarlet aril or mace from the nut, which is then dried.

Cloves and nutmeg are, surprisingly, rarely used in cooking in the Moluccas. Although a little grated nutmeg may be added to a rich beef soup, nutmeg and cloves are regarded more as medicinal plants here and were too valuable to be eaten! Nutmeg fruit, the fleshy covering of the hard nut which is used as a spice, is however pickled and eaten as a snack. It is also the traveler's friend, considered good for seasickness, while cloves are the universal cure for a toothache.

While these are indigenous spices, some of the other spices used in Indonesian cooking came from the Middle East or India, such as fibrous cardamom pods containing tiny black seeds known in the Middle Ages as "grains of paradise," native to India and Sri Lanka. True cinnamon grows in Sri Lanka, while the coarse bark generally sold as cinnamon in Indonesia and other parts of Southeast Asia really comes from the bark of a type of cassia tree. Coarser, darker in color and less expensive, it adds a robust flavor to some meat dishes.

The most widely used spice in Indonesia is coriander, a small round beige seed with a faintly orange flavor. This spice was known to the ancient Greeks and is found throughout the Middle East and India, as well as in Southeast Asia. Coriander is commonly partnered with peppercorns, garlic and coconut to flavor dishes, especially in Java. Another spice often used with coriander is cumin, an elongated seed that looks and smells a little like caraway. A similar spice, fennel, is fatter, whiter and sweeter in fragrance than cumin.

Both black and white peppercorns, each of which has its distinct flavor, are used in most parts of the archipelago. Peppercorns are the berry of a vine native to the Malabar coast of India, brought to Indonesia many centuries ago. Black peppercorns are the dried ripe berry with the skin intact, while white peppercorns have had the skins removed.

Coastal areas of Indonesia, which were major trading centers (such as the eastern seaboard of Sumatra, which saw Arab and India traders long before the Chinese and Europeans arrived, and the west and north coasts of Java), use a wider range of spices and seasonings than areas that had little contact with the outside world. While some Sumatran dishes, for example, may call for as many as six or seven different spices and at least as many roots, herbs and seasonings, a dish from a remote island in eastern Indonesia might be flavored only with turmeric and salt, or cooked without any seasoning and eaten with a dipping sauce or spicy sambal.

OPPOSITE: Boats fashioned entirely from cloves (the dried bud of a tree native to just five islands in eastern Indonesia) are a popular souvenir item today in the Spice Islands. The majority of Indonesia's clove crop today goes up in smoke in the form of clove-scented cigarettes. RIGHT: Chilies, brought to Asia from the Americas by the Spanish four centuries ago, are an indispensible ingredient in Indonesian cuisine, whether whole or ground into a fiery paste. PAGES 12 AND 13: Every stage of the rice cycle is accompanied by rituals, some simple, others elaborate to ensure a bountiful harvest.

An Invitation to a Feast
How an Indonesian Meal is Composed and Eaten

"*Silahkan makan*" is the polite Indonesian invitation that precedes any meal served to guests (and a phrase that foreigners should always wait for before beginning to eat any food or snack served by their Indonesian hosts). But in most homes throughout the archipelago, when guests are not present, meals are usually an informal affair and often eaten alone. Millions of Indonesian women are up before dawn, when the fragrance of cooking fires wafts through the freshness of the early morning on their return from market with the day's provisions. Before the task of cooking begins, there will be a simple breakfast, often some leftovers from the night before, perhaps a few sticky cakes from the market, a bowl of noodles or a simple plate of fried rice.

The most popular staple food is rice (although there are variations in many regions) and Indonesians eat surprisingly large amounts of it, together with many side dishes and condiments. Only small amounts of these savory dishes—which may include fish, poultry, meat, eggs, vegetables, tofu or tempeh— are eaten. Variety rather than volume is the name of the game, Indonesians preferring to enjoy just a little of four or five dishes rather than large helpings of only one or two.

Condiments are just as important as the savory dishes and usually include a chili-hot sambal as well as something to provide a crunchy contrast. This could be deep-fried tempeh, peanuts, deep-fried tiny fish (*ikan teri*), *krupuk* (wafers made of tapioca flour seasoned with fish, shrimp or bitter *melinjo* nuts and then deep-fried), a fried coconut concoction such as *serundeng* or fried peanut wafers (*rempeyek*).

The rice and side dishes are normally cooked early in the day, immediately after a trip to the market or with items gathered from the garden. Many meals, especially in the more remote areas of this far-flung archipelago, are extremely simple and may consist of the local staple plus a little dried fish and chili sambal with, perhaps, some deep-fried shallots or a drizzling of sweet black soy sauce (*kecap manis*) with some chopped herbs or lime juice.

The prepared food is usually set on a table in the kitchen protected from insects by conical food covers made of woven pandanus leaves or plastic mesh. Members of the family help themselves to whatever they want whenever they feel hungry during the day, or may take a container of food to the fields or office to be eaten at midday. Evening meals, taken at the end of the day, are often based on food leftover from the main midday meal, with one or two extra dishes cooked if necessary.

As the food is often eaten some time after it has been prepared, it is usually served at room temperature. Modern homes in the towns and cities often have rice cookers, to keep cooked rice warm for several hours.

Where meals are communal, the rice and all the accompanying dishes are placed in the middle of the table or on a mat on the floor and everyone helps themselves to whatever they want. It is considered impolite to pile one's plate with food at the first serving; just a little will do, as there's plenty of opportunity to take more food as the meal progresses.

Indonesians traditionally eat with the right hand (the left is considered unclean by Muslims), although serving spoons are used to transfer the food to individual plates or bowls from the serving dishes. (Never use a spoon or fork that you are eating from to take food from a communal serving dish, as this is considered unclean!) Most homes and restaurants provide a spoon and fork, while chopsticks can be expected in Chinese restaurants.

In more affluent homes, the choice of dishes to accompany the rice is made with a view to achieving a blend of flavors and textures. If one of the savory dishes has a rich, coconut-milk gravy, this will be offset by a dry dish with a sharper flavor. There may well be a pungent *sambal goreng* (food fried with a spicy chili seasoning), but this will be balanced with other mild or sweet dishes using *kecap manis* (sweet black soy sauce) or palm sugar.

Part of the joy of cooking Indonesian food is planning the range of dishes. Many of them can be prepared well in advance, so once the guests arrive, you can relax and enjoy their company.

ABOVE: Gorgeously attired Buginese girls in Southern Sulawesi enjoy a meal where, in typical Indonesian style, rice and side dishes are placed in the center of the table for everyone to help themselves. RIGHT: A back lane in Ubud is decorated for a temple festival. The tall bamboo poles by the roadside are known as *penjor*, and are symbols of prosperity.

The Indonesian Kitchen
A combination of simplicity and practicality

One of the many surprising aspects of Indonesia is the way such delicious foods—often complex blendings of herbs, spices and seasonings—come out of the simplest of kitchens. The gleaming modern designer kitchen with tiled surfaces, electrical appliances and hot and cold running water is unknown to the majority of Indonesians. Kitchens are functional rather than aesthetic, with meals cooked over a wood fire or a *kompor*, a kerosene burner. In urban areas, gas burners fueled by LPG are increasingly used.

Preparing Indonesian food in your kitchen does require a fairly complex array of ingredients, but the number of utensils needed is not that great (see following section). First and foremost you need something to grind or crush the seasonings (*bumbu*) that form the basis of countless Indonesian dishes and are also used as condiments or sambals. In Indonesia, a saucer-shaped **mortar** together with a **pestle**, both made of volcanic stone, are used for this task. Unlike neighboring Malaysia and Thailand, where ingredients are pounded with a pestle inside a deep mortar, the Indonesian cook rubs or grinds ingredients with a backwards and forwards motion across the stone, which is broad and slightly rounded but almost flat.

Although a mortar and pestle is very useful for dealing with small amounts of ingredients, most modern cooks will find a f**ood processor**, **blender** or **spice grinder** the easiest way to prepare the basic spice paste or *rempah*. Small spice grinder attachments to food processors or blenders are widely available now and very handy for grinding small amounts of spices.

Also important is a **chopping board** and **cleaver**. This duo performs a myriad of tasks: chopping up chicken into the required size; cutting vegetables; finely mincing meat or fish in the absence of a food processor. The flat side of the cleaver is used to bruise lemongrass, cardamom pods or garlic (to remove the garlic skin), and so on. In Asia, a thick cross-section of a tree trunk is used as a chopping board; this type of board is durable and functional. Choose the biggest board available, with a cleaver that has a blade 3–4 in (7–10 cm) wide.

A **wok**, basically a conical frying pan, is infinitely preferable to a frying pan for many dishes. Known as a *kuali* (or, in Javanese, *wajan*), this versatile utensil is practical for deep-frying (it uses less oil) and also allows the right amount of evaporation for many dishes which begin with a large amount of liquid and finish with a thick sauce. When choosing a wok, avoid aluminum or non-stick types and try to get one that is large and quite thick.

A heavy cast iron wok that won't tip over easily is preferable, or best of all, the Rolls Royce of woks, which is made of a non-stick alloy that will not scratch when metal scoops are used. To partner your wok, a **metal spatula** and a **perforated ladle** for lifting out deep-fried food, are useful. Indonesian cooks also use an assortment of wooden or coconut husk spoons for stirring.

It is important not to use aluminum or cast iron saucepans for cooking Indonesian food. Many recipes contain acidic ingredients, such as tamarind juice or lime, or coconut milk, and using aluminum or cast iron will result in a discolored sauce or cause a chemical reaction. Choose either stainless steel, glass or enameled saucepans.

One item widely used in Indonesian cooking is seldom easily available outside the tropics. This is the multi-purpose **banana leaf**, used for wrapping foods for grilling, steaming, or placing directly onto hot coals (see page 19). Just to give some idea of the versatility of the banana leaf, one Indonesian cooking manual illustrates 24 different ways of wrapping foods in banana leaves, depending on the contents and the particular style of preparation! If you are able to obtain banana leaves, wipe them clean and cut to the required size. Hold the leaf directly over a gas flame or pour boiling water over it in a basin until it softens before using it to wrap foods. Aluminum foil can be substituted, but for a texture that is closer to that obtained by using the banana leaf, wrap foods in parchment paper first, then in foil. Bundles of banana leaf-wrapped foods are often steamed, usually inside conical rattan steaming baskets used to steam rice. The most practical approach in a Western kitchen is to buy a two-tiered Chinese **bamboo steamer** with a cover. This steamer sits inside a wok above the boiling water. The bamboo is ideal, as it absorbs moisture rather than letting it fall back into the food. Rinse and dry the steamer and lid thoroughly after use before storing.

An alternative to the bamboo steamer is a **perforated metal** disc that sits inside a wok above the boiling water; however, this will not hold as much food as a two-tiered steamer, and you will need to find a convex lid that fits over your wok.

OPPOSITE: The traditional mortar and pestle made of volcanic lava stone is commonly found in Indonesian homes, an essential tool for preparing the spice pastes that are a part of almost every Indonesian recipe. The basic spice paste or *rempah* consists of shallots, ginger, galangal, lemongrass and candlenuts, with other spices or herbs often added as well.

Cooking Methods

Preparing the all-important spice pastes, rice and coconut milk

Indonesian food is prepared in a variety of ways: pan-fried or deep-fried, grilled over hot coals, simmered, steamed and even—in remote areas of Irian Jaya—baked in an earth oven as in Polynesia.

It is essential to master the art of preparing the **basic spice paste** or *rempah* used to season so many dishes. Indonesian cooks use a grinding stone; ingredients are peeled if necessary and, where relevant, sliced or chopped into small pieces before being ground. If you are using a blender or food processor, the order of processing the spices is much the same as for a grinding stone and pestle, but you will probably need to add some liquid to keep the mixture turning inside the processor during the blending process. If the spice paste is to be fried first in some hot oil, add just a little of the specified amount of oil to the food processor. If the spice paste is to be simmered in either coconut milk, stock or water, add a little of this liquid instead.

The order to be followed when grinding or processing spice paste ingredients is important. Grind hard items first: dried spices, nuts and tough fibrous roots or leaves, such as galangal and lemongrass. When these are fine, add softer roots, such as ginger and fresh or soaked dried chilies. Process until fine, then add ingredients that are full of moisture, such as shallots and garlic. Finally, add soft, crumbly or liquid ingredients like dried shrimp paste, palm sugar and tamarind juice, and process to mix well. If the mixture is sticking to the sides, you may have to turn off the machine and shake the container or open it and push the ingredients to the center using a spatula.

The spice paste is then either fried in oil or simmered in liquid in the wok. If it is to be fried, put it in oil over low to moderate heat and fry, stirring from time to time, until fragrant. This takes from 5–7 minutes. Often, pieces of meat or poultry are added to the spice paste and stir-fried until they are well coated and the color has changed. Coconut milk is frequently added at this stage and the liquid brought to a simmer before the heat is lowered and the food cooked until done.

When cooking with **coconut milk**, it is important to prevent it from curdling or breaking apart. Stir the milk frequently, lifting it up with a large spoon or ladle and pouring it back into the pan or wok. Once the milk is simmering, reduce the heat and do not cover the pan. Thick coconut milk should be added at the final stages of cooking a dish to thicken and enrich the flavor. Stir constantly while heating and do not allow the coconut to boil.

Rice, the staff of life

Rice, the physical mainstay of millions of Indonesians, is far more than just a staple food. The plant is perceived to have a soul or spirit and is therefore subject to many ritual observances during growth and harvesting. Although there are dozens of varieties of rice in Indonesia, the most common fall into two basic categories: **long-grain polished white rice** and **glutinous rice**. The former is eaten as a staple with almost every meal, while glutinous rice is used to make desserts, cakes and snacks that are eaten on special occasions. Glutinous or sticky rice (*ketan* or *pulut*) is either white or purplish-black (*pulut hitam*), with a wonderfully nutty flavor.

Cooking rice is a subject that often arouses controversy, and if you already have a favorite method, stick with it. Whatever method is used, it is essential to first wash the rice to remove any dirt and starch clinging to the grains; failure to do this may result in soggy rice. Put the rice into a saucepan, fill it halfway with water, rub the grains for a few seconds, then pour off the water. Repeat this step as many times as necessary until the water runs clear. Drain well.

The absorbency of rice depends on the variety and its age, with older rice absorbing more liquid. Cooking times depend on the type and weight of your saucepan, and the heat of your stove. The following absorption method is used by millions throughout Asia.

Plain Rice (*Nasi Putih*)

Measure out about of $1/2$ cup (100 g) of uncooked rice grains per person and wash thoroughly. Place into a heavy-bottomed saucepan with enough water to cover the rice and come up to the level of the first joint on your forefinger (about $3/4$ in/$1 1/2$ cm). Cover the pan and bring to a boil over high heat. Set the lid slightly to one side, lower the heat and simmer until all the water is absorbed and dimples or "craters" appear in the top of the rice, about 10 minutes. Reduce the heat to the absolute minimum, cover the pan and leave the rice to cook for at least another 10 minutes. Remove the lid, fluff up the rice with a fork (do not stir before this), wipe any condensation off the lid and cover the pan again. Set aside until required. The rice should keep warm for at least another 15–20 minutes.

LEFT: A traditional volcanic stone mortar and pestle is used to grind the basic spice paste or *rempah*, but a modern food processor does the job far more quickly and effortlessly.

Wrapping Foods in Banana Leaves

The muli-purpose food wrapper

Steaming, grilling or frying foods that have been wrapped in banana leaves imparts a subtle fragrance to them. Before wrapping, cut the leaves into rectangles, rinse them well and then scald them in a basin by pouring boiling water over them. This softens the leaves so that they bend easily without cracking when you fold them.

Simple Banana Leaf Rolls (Pepes)

Step 1: Place the ingredients in a cylinder along a piece of clean leaf.

Step 2: Roll the leaf up around the filling.

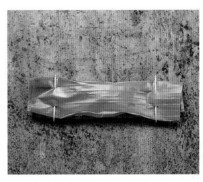

Step 3: Secure both ends of the roll with toothpicks.

Double-wrapped Banana Leaf Packets

Step 1: Place the ingredients in the center of a leaf and fold one side in with your index finger.

Step 2: Repeat on the other side.

Step 3: Fold one folded side over to the front and the other to the back.

Step 4: Repeat on the other side to firmly enclose the contents.

Step 5: Wrap the bundle with another long and narrow strip of leaf.

Step 6: Secure with a toothpick at the top.

root before grinding as it is tough. Galangal is also available dried, frozen and packed in water, but try to get the fresh root whenever possible as it is far more fragrant.

Garlic chives (*kucai*), sometimes referred to as Chinese chives, have flattened leaves and resemble thin spring onions. They have a strong garlicky flavor and are often added to noodle or stir-fried vegetable dishes during the final stages of cooking. Substitute spring onions, although their flavor is more mild.

Jicama (*bangkuang*) is a crunchy and juicy white tuber that is peeled and

eaten raw, sliced and served with rock salt or dressing as a refreshing snack. Look for it in the produce section of supermarkets.

Kaffir lime leaves (*daun jeruk purut*) are added whole to curries, or finely shredded and added to salads, giving them a wonderfully tangy flavor. They are commonly used in Indonesian and other Southeast Asia cuisines, and are available frozen or dried in Asian food stores. Frozen leaves are more flavorful than dried ones.

Kencur, sometimes mistakenly called lesser galangal, is also known as zedoary. *Kencur* has a unique, camphor-like flavor and should be used sparingly. It must be rinsed and the

skin scraped off before using. Dried *kencur* should be soaked in boiling water for 30 minutes to soften before use. If using ground *kencur*, substitute $1/2$–1 teaspoon of the powder for 1 in ($2^1/_2$ cm) of the fresh root. Try to use the fresh root whenever possible as it is more fragrant.

Krupuk are dried crackers made from bits of shrimp, fish, vegetables and nuts mixed with various types of flour to make a very popular snack in Indonesia. They must be thoroughly dried in the sun or in an oven set on very low before deep-frying in very hot oil for a few seconds, when they puff up spectacularly and become crispy. Store fried *krupuk* in an airtight container.

Yellow wheat noodles
(*mie*)

Flat rice stick noodles
(*kway teow*)

Dried rice vermicelli
(*beehoon*)

Dried glass noodles
(*tanghoon*)

Noodles are a universal favorite in Indonesia which the Indonesians have enthusiastically adopted from the Chinese. Both fresh and dried noodles made from either wheat, rice or mung bean flour are found. **Yellow wheat noodles** (*mie*) are spaghetti-like noodles made from wheat flour and egg. In Indonesia they generally come dried in packets, like ramen. **Flat rice stick noodles** (*kway teow*) are ribbon-like noodles of varying widths, used in soups or fried. They generally come dried in packets. **Dried rice vermicelli** (*beehoon*) are very fine rice threads that must be plunged into boiling water to soften before use. **Dried glass noodles**, made from mung beans, are fine white strands that are generally used in soups. They are also called "cellophane" or "transparent" noodles, both accurate descriptions of their appearance after soaking. Both fresh and dried noodles should be blanched in boiling water before cooking to rinse and revive them—use a pair of long chopsticks to keep them from sticking together.

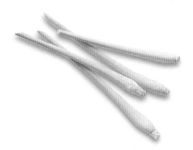

Rice flour is made from ground uncooked rice grains. It is used to make the dough or batter for many desserts.

Sago flour is made from ground sago and imparts a very subtle flavor and delicate texture to desserts. Sold in plastic packets in Asian specialty shops.

Lemongrass (*serai*) is a fragrant, lemony stalk that is either bruised and used whole in soups or curries, or sliced and ground as part of a basic spice mix. It is usually sold in bunches of 3 to 4 stems in supermarkets. The tough outer layers should be peeled away and only the inner part of the thick lower third of the stem is used. Always slice the stem before grinding to get a smooth paste.

Palm sugar (*gula jawa*) is sold as a solid block or cylinder of sugar made from the sap of the coconut or arenga sugar palm. It varies in color from gold to light brown and has a faint caramel taste. It is used to make Palm Sugar Syrup (page 104). To measure, hard palm sugar should be shaved, grated or melted in a microwave oven. Substitute dark brown sugar.

Salam leaves, from the cassia family, are used in the same way bay leaves are used in Western cooking—to add a complex earthy fragrance to dishes. If unavailable, omit them from the recipe altogether. Do not substitute with bay leaves as the flavor is totally different.

Limes of several types are used in Indonesia. Round yellow-skinned limes (*jeruk nipis*) are slightly larger than a golf ball. The small, dark green calamansi limes (*jeruk limau*) are used for their fragrant juice and rind. Other types of limes may also be used.

Pandanus leaves impart a subtle fragrance and a green hue to a range of Indonesian dishes. They are usually tied in a knot and then added to a liquid recipe. Bottled pandanus extract can be substituted in desserts, but if fresh or dried pandanus leaves are not available, omit them from savory dishes. Vanilla essence may be substituted in dessert recipes.

Star anise (*bunga lawang*) is an 8-pointed dried pod encasing shiny black seeds with a strong aniseed flavor. The whole spice is usually used when cooking and is discarded before serving. Whole star anise keeps for a year in an airtight container.

Mung bean flour (*tepong hoen kwe*) is sold in paper-wrapped cylinders—sometimes, the flour is colored pink or green and the paper wrapper correspondingly colored. It gives a more delicate texture to desserts than rice flour.

Nutmeg (*pala*) is the inner kernel of the fruit of the nutmeg tree. The lacy covering on the nutmeg is another spice—mace. Always grate whole nutmeg just before using as the powdered spice loses its fragrance quickly. Whole nutmegs keep almost indefinitely.

Soy sauce is brewed from soybeans and wheat fermented with salt. It is salty and used as a table dip and cooking seasoning. Black soy sauce is denser and less salty than regular soy sauce. It adds a smoky flavor to dishes. Sweet Indonesian soy sauce (*kecap manis*) is much sweeter and thicker than normal soy sauce. It has palm sugar and cane molasses added. Sweet Chinese soy sauce may be substituted or you can just add dark brown sugar to normal soy, or you can try to find Indonesian *kecap manis* if you can, because it has a distinctive flavor.

Sweet Indonesian soy sauce
(*kecap manis*)

| Firm tofu | Pressed tofu | Deep-fried tofu |

Tamarind (*asam jawa*) is a fruit that is often sold dried in Indonesia, still encased inside its long narrow tree pod. Outside of Indonesia, the pulp is more often sold in jars and packets already shelled, but sill containing some fibers and seeds. It is used as a souring agent in many dishes. To obtain **tamarind juice**, mash 1 part pulp in 2 parts warm water and strain. Discard the seeds or fibers. If using already cleaned tamarind pulp, slightly reduce the amounts called for in the recipes. The dried pulp keeps indefinitely in an airtight container.

Tapioca leaves are the tender young leaves from the top of the tapioca or cassava plant. They are boiled and eaten as a green vegetable in many parts of Asia. Substitute spinach or water spinach (*kangkung*).

Tempeh or fermented soybean cakes, a Javanese creation, are made of compressed, lightly fermented soybeans with a delicious nutty flavor. They can be fried, steamed or baked and are a rich source of protein, riboflavin, calcium and iron. They are low in cholesterol and sodium and are increasingly popular with health enthusiasts. They are sold in most health food stores and Asian specialty shops—plain, marinated or smoked. Look for them in the refrigerator or freezer section.

Tofu is rich in protein and amazingly versatile. **Firm tofu** holds its shape well when cut or cooked and has a strong, slightly sour taste. **Pressed tofu** (often confusingly labelled as firm tofu) has much of the moisture extracted and is therefore much firmer in texture and excellent for stir-fries. Refrigerate fresh tofu immersed in water. Slices of **deep-fried tofu** (*tau foo pok*) are sold ready-made in supermarkets and wet markets, and may be sliced or cubed and added to stir-fried dishes and soups.

Turmeric (*kunyit*) is a root similar to ginger but with a bright yellow to orange color and a strong woody flavor. Turmeric has antiseptic and astringent qualities, and stains permanently, so scrub your knife blade, hands and chopping board immediately after handling. Purchase fresh turmeric root as needed as the flavor fades after a few days. Substitute 1 teaspoon ground turmeric for 1 in ($2^1/_2$ cm) of the fresh root. **Turmeric leaves** are used as a herb, particularly in Sumatra. There is no substitute.

Water spinach (*kangkung*) is a nutritious, leafy vegetable also known as morning glory or water convolvulus. The leaves and tender tips are often stir-fried. Spinach is a good substitute.

Whitebait (*ikan teri*) are baby fish ranging from 1 to 2 in (2 to 5 cm) in length. They are usually sold in Asia salted and sun-dried. Discard the heads and black intestinal tracts before using. If possible, buy them split, cleaned and ready for use. They are usually quite salty, so taste any dish using whitebait before adding more salt, or soak them for a longer time to reduce the saltiness.

Authentic Indonesian Recipes

Portions

In Indonesia, as in most Asian countries, food is seldom served in individual portions. Large serving bowls of rice and other main dishes are normally placed on the table for diners to help themselves family style. Small amounts of the main dishes are eaten with copious amounts of fragrant, fluffy boiled rice. It is thus difficult to estimate the exact number of portions each recipe will provide. As a general rule, however, the recipes in this book will serve 4 to 6 people as part of a meal with rice and 3 or 4 other dishes.

Indonesian seasonings

The quantities of chilies, sweet Indonesian soy sauce (*kecap manis*) and dried shrimp paste (*trasi*) given in the following recipes are to be taken as approximate guides, not absolute measures. Bear in mind that you can always increase the amount of seasonings later just before serving, whereas if you overdo it in the initial stages, you cannot reduce the seasonings later.

Pickles and sambals

The pickles and sambals given on pages 31 to 34 can usually be stored in a well-sealed glass jar in a refrigerator for a week. Some of them, like Acar Segar, Serundeng and Sambal Trasi (a sambal is a chili sauce or spicy relish) can be served as appetizers or side dishes with a meal. It is not unusual to find bowls of different pickles and sambals on the dining table in an Indonesian home.

Ingredients

Many Indonesian ingredients are now available in well-stocked supermarkets outside of Indonesia—like dried shrimp paste (*trasi*), black shrimp paste (*petis*), *kencur* (zedoary), coconut cream and lemongrass. The names on the packages may be different, however, as similar or identical ingredients from Singapore, Malaysia, Thailand or Vietnam are called by different names in those countries. Check the ingredient listings on pages 22 to 27 for these alternative names and look for ingredients that are more difficult to find in Asian specialty shops.

Tips on grinding spices

When using a mortar and pestle or blender to prepare spice pastes, it helps to peel and slice all the ingredients before grinding them. Grind tougher ingredients first before grinding the softer ones. If using a blender, add a little liquid (oil, coconut milk or water, depending on the recipe) to keep the mixture turning. Be sure not to overload the blender—if the quantity is too large, pulse them in batches and grind each batch before starting the next. If you have to roast some ingredients before grinding, which is usually the case with dried shrimp paste (*trasi*), allow them to cool before grinding. Spice pastes need only be ground coarsely—not to a purée. Store unused spice pastes in plastic wrap or an airtight container in the refrigerator or freezer.

Time estimates

Time estimates are for preparation and cooking, and are based on the assumption that a food processor or blender will be used.

Pickles, Sambals and Dipping Sauces

Cucumber Pickles

1 medium cucumber, peeled, halved lengthwise, deseeded and sliced
1 tablespoon white vinegar
$2^1/_2$ tablespoons sugar
1 teaspoon salt
$2^1/_2$ tablespoons hot water

Place the sliced cucumber in a bowl. Combine the vinegar, sugar, salt and hot water in another bowl, then add to the cucumber and toss well. Set aside to cure for 1 hour before serving. This pickle keeps for a week in a jar in the refrigerator.

Makes 1 cup
Preparation time: 10 mins + 1 hour to cure

Mixed Vegetable Pickles
Acar Segar

1 small cucumber, peeled, deseeded and cut into matchsticks
1 small carrot, peeled and cut into matchsticks
8 shallots, peeled and quartered
$3/_4$ cup (180 ml) water
3 tablespoons white vinegar
1 tablespoon sugar
1 teaspoon salt

Place the sliced vegetables in a bowl. In another bowl, combine the water, vinegar, sugar and salt, then add to the vegetables and mix well. Set aside to cure for 2 or 3 days in the refrigerator before serving. This pickle keeps for 2 weeks in the refrigerator.

Makes 2 cups
Preparation time: 20 mins + 2 to 3 days to cure

Spicy Pickles with Basil

1 small cucumber, peeled and sliced
$1/2$ cup (25 g) bean sprouts, seed coats and tails discarded, blanched
2 shallots, peeled and thinly sliced
1 red finger-length chili, deseeded and sliced
1–2 bird's-eye chilies, deseeded and sliced
2 sprigs Asian basil, minced
3 tablespoons coarsely ground raw almonds, cashews or candlenuts
$1/4$ teaspoon dried shrimp paste (*trasi*), dry-roasted (page 23)
2 tablespoons freshly squeezed lime or lemon juice
$1/4$ teaspoon sugar
$1/4$ teaspoon salt
1–2 tablespoons warm water

1 Place the sliced cucumber and bean sprouts in a bowl, then spread the sliced shallot, chilies and basil on top.
2 Combine the remaining ingredients in another bowl and mix well to make a thick sauce. Drizzle the sauce over the vegetables, mix well and set aside to cure for 2 to 3 hours. If storing the pickles, keep the vegetables and sauce separate. This pickle keeps for a week in the refrigerator.

Makes $1^1/2$ cups
Preparation time: 20 mins + 2 to 3 hours to cure

Pickled Green Chilies

$1^1/2$ tablespoons sugar
2 tablespoons white vinegar
1 teaspoon salt
$2^1/2$ tablespoons warm water
10 finger-length green chilies, deseeded and sliced

Combine the sugar, vinegar, salt and warm water in a bowl. Add the sliced chili and mix well. Set aside to cure for 2 to 3 hours, then serve in small bowls. This pickle keeps for a week in the refrigerator.

Makes 1 cup
Preparation time: 15 mins + 2 to 3 hours to cure

Pickled Shallots

2 tablespoons white vinegar
$1^1/2$ tablespoons sugar
1 teaspoon salt
3 tablespoons warm water
20 shallots, peeled and sliced
1 red finger-length chili, deseeded and sliced

Combine the vinegar, sugar, salt and warm water in a bowl. Add the sliced shallot and chili, and mix well. Set aside to cure for 2 to 3 hours, then serve in small bowls. This pickle keeps for a week in the refrigerator.

Makes 1 cup
Preparation time: 20 mins + 2 to 3 hours to cure

Green Mango Sambal

1 unripe mango (about 8 oz/ 250 g), peeled and pitted, flesh finely diced
1 teaspoon salt
1 red finger-length chili, deseeded
5 shallots, peeled
$1/2$ teaspoon dried shrimp paste (*trasi*), dry-roasted (page 23)
1 sprig Asian basil, minced
2 tablespoons oil

1 Sprinkle the mango with the salt, mix well and set aside for 10 to 15 minutes in a colander to drain. Place the mango in a dry cloth and squeeze out as much liquid as you can.
2 Grind the chili, shallots and dried shrimp paste to a smooth paste in a mortar or blender, adding a little oil to keep the mixture turning. Add the basil and oil to the ground mixture and mix well, then add this mixture to the mango and toss lightly. Serve immediately.

Makes $1^1/2$ cups
Preparation time: 15 mins

Diced Water Chestnut or Jicama Sambal

10–12 fresh or canned water chestnuts or 1 small jicama (*bangkuang*), peeled and diced
2–3 red finger-length chilies, deseeded and sliced
2 cloves garlic, peeled
$1/2$ teaspoon dried shrimp paste (*trasi*), dry-roasted (page 23)
$1/2$ teaspoon salt
$1^1/2$ tablespoons freshly squeezed lime or lemon juice
2 sprigs Asian basil

1 Place the water chestnuts or jicama and half of the chilies in a bowl.
2 Grind the remaining chilies with the garlic, dried shrimp paste, salt and lime or lemon juice to a coarse paste in a mortar or blender. Add the ground mixture to the vegetables and mix well. Garnish with the basil and serve.

Makes 2 cups
Preparation time: 30 mins

Shallot Sambal

2 tablespoons oil
15 shallots, peeled and sliced
2–3 red finger-length chilies, deseeded and sliced
4 cloves garlic, sliced
$1/2$ teaspoon salt
2 teaspoons dried shrimp paste (*trasi*), dry-roasted (page 23)
2 teaspoons freshly squeezed lime or lemon juice

1 Heat the oil in a wok and stir-fry all the ingredients, except the lime or lemon juice, over high heat for 1 to 2 minutes. Remove from the heat and set aside to cool.
2 Add the lime juice and mix well, then serve in small bowls. This sambal keeps in the refrigerator for up to a week.

Makes $3/4$ cup
Preparation time: 20 mins
Cooking time: 2 mins

Sambal Kecap
Sweet Soy Sauce Sambal

3–4 shallots, peeled and sliced
1 red finger-length chili, deseeded
  and sliced
2 tablespoons sweet Indonesian soy
  sauce (*kecap manis*)

Combine all the ingredients, mix
well and serve in a small bowl.

Makes 1/2 cup
Preparation time: 5 mins

Dried Shrimp and Vegetable Sambal

3 candlenuts or macadamia nuts
1/2 in (1 cm) fresh galangal (*laos*),
  peeled and sliced
2 red finger-length chilies, deseeded
5 shallots, peeled
3 cloves garlic, peeled
1 tablespoon oil
1 cup (120 g) dried shrimp, soaked
  for 15 minutes, then drained and
  ground coarsely in a mortar or blender
1 teaspoon dark brown sugar
1 cup (250 ml) thick coconut milk
1 *salam* leaf
1/4 teaspoon salt
8 oz (250 g) cabbage or zucchini,
  peeled and sliced

1 Grind the candlenuts, galangal,
chilies, shallots and garlic to a
smooth paste in a mortar or blender,
adding a little oil if necessary to
keep the mixture turning.
2 Heat the oil in a wok over medium
high heat and stir-fry the ground
mixture until fragrant, 2 to 3 minutes.
Add the dried shrimp and sugar, and
continue to stir-fry for 2 more minutes.
3 Add the coconut milk and *salam*
leaf, mix well and season with the
salt. Bring the mixture almost to a
boil, then reduce the heat, add the
cabbage or zucchini and simmer,
stirring from time to time until just
tender, about 15 minutes.

Makes 2 1/2 cups
Preparation time: 30 mins
Cooking time: 25 mins

Sambal Trasi
Chili Sauce with Shrimp Paste

4 red finger-length chilies, deseeded
1 tablespoon dried shrimp paste
  (*trasi*), dry-roasted (page 23)
1 tablespoon shaved palm sugar or
  dark brown sugar
1 tablespoon freshly squeezed lime
  or lemon juice

Grind all the ingredients to a smooth
paste in a mortar or blender. For a
more fiery sambal, substitute bird's-
eye chilies for the finger-length chilies.

Makes 1 cup
Preparation time: 10 mins

Peanut Sambal with Tamarind

1 tablespoon oil
5 shallots, peeled and thinly sliced
2 cloves garlic, sliced
4 red finger-length chilies, or 2 bird's-
  eye chilies, deseeded and sliced
1 1/2 cups (225 g) roasted unsalted
  peanuts, skins discarded, coarsely
  ground in a mortar or blender
1 teaspoon dried shrimp paste (*trasi*),
  dry-roasted (page 23)
2 tablespoons tamarind juice (page 26)
4 tablespoons sweet Indonesian soy
  sauce (*kecap manis*)
1 teaspoon salt

1 Heat the oil in a wok over medium
heat and stir-fry the sliced shallot
and garlic until fragrant and golden
brown, 2 to 3 minutes.
2 Add the sliced chili, peanuts,
shrimp paste, tamarind juice and
sweet soy sauce, mix well and bring
to a boil. Reduce the heat to low
and simmer for 1 to 2 minutes, then
season with the salt and remove
from the heat. Serve in small bowls
as a condiment for grilled fish and
meat with slices of green tomato
and cucumber. This sambal keeps
for a week in the refrigerator.

Makes 1 cup
Preparation time: 20 mins
Cooking time: 10 mins

Sambal Tauco
Yellow Bean Sauce Sambal

1/4 cup (70 g) yellow bean sauce
  (*tauco*) or miso
1/4 cup (60 ml) thick coconut milk

Spice Paste
3 green finger-length chilies,
  deseeded
4 shallots, peeled
3 cloves garlic, peeled
2 tablespoons oil
1 stalk lemongrass, thick bottom third
  only, outer layers discarded, inner
  part bruised
2 *salam* leaves
1 tablespoon tamarind juice (page 26)
1 teaspoon shaved palm sugar or
  dark brown sugar

1 Make the Spice Paste by grinding
the chilies, shallots and garlic to a
smooth paste in a mortar or blender,
adding a little oil if necessary to
keep the mixture turning. Heat the
oil in a wok over medium high heat
and stir-fry the ground paste with all
the other ingredients until fragrant,
3 to 5 minutes.
2 Add the yellow bean sauce or miso
and stir-fry for 1 more minute.
Reduce the heat to low, add the
coconut milk, mix well and simmer
for 3 to 4 minutes, stirring until the
sambal is thickened. Remove from
the heat and set aside to cool, then
serve in small bowls. This sambal
keeps for a week in the refrigerator.

Makes 1 cup
Preparation time: 15 mins
Cooking time: 10 mins

Sambal Rujak
Rujak Sauce

1/2 cup (100 g) shaved palm sugar or
  dark brown sugar
1/2 cup (125 ml) water
1/4 cup (60 ml) tamarind juice (page
  26)
1 teaspoon dried shrimp paste (*trasi*),
  dry-roasted (page 23)
3–4 bird's-eye chilies, left whole
1/2 teaspoon salt
1/2 cup (125 ml) water

1 In a saucepan, bring the sugar
and water to a boil, then reduce
the heat to low and simmer until
the syrup is thickened, about 10
minutes.
2 Add all the other ingredients, stir
well, increase the heat to medium
and bring the mixture to a boil.
Reduce the heat to low again and
simmer for about 5 minutes, then
remove from the heat and set aside
to cool. Strain the sambal before
serving.

Makes 1 cup
Preparation time: 10 mins
Cooking time: 20 mins

Crispy Fried Shallots or Fried Garlic

10–15 shallots or 30 cloves garlic
1 cup (250 ml) oil

1 Peel and thinly slice the shallots or
garlic, then pat dry with paper towels.
2 Heat the oil in a wok over medium
low heat and stir-fry the sliced shallot
or garlic until golden brown and
crispy, 3 to 5 minutes. Do not allow
them to burn or they will taste bitter.
Drain well using a wire mesh sieve
and allow to cool completely, then
store in an airtight container. Reserve
the **Shallot** or **Garlic Oil** for frying or
seasoning other dishes.

Makes 1 1/2 cups
Preparation time: 20 mins
Cooking time: 5 mins

Sambal Kacang
Peanut Sauce for Satay

1 cup (150 g) roasted unsalted
  peanuts, skins discarded
3 cloves garlic, peeled
1 in (2 1/2 cm) fresh *kencur* root,
  peeled and sliced
2–3 bird's-eye chilies, deseeded
1 kaffir lime leaf
3 tablespoons sweet Indonesian soy
  sauce (*kecap manis*)
1/2 teaspoon salt
1 1/2 cups (375 ml) water
1 teaspoon freshly squeezed lime or
  lemon juice
1 tablespoon Crispy Fried Shallots
  (see recipe on this page)

1 Grind the peanuts, garlic, *kencur*
and chilies coarsely in a mortar or
blender.
2 Combine the ground ingredients
with all the other ingredients (except
the lime or lemon juice and Crispy
Fried Shallots) in a saucepan, mix
well and simmer over medium heat
for 20 to 15 minutes, stirring constantly to prevent the sauce from
burning. Add more water as needed
to keep the sauce a thick consistency.
Remove from the heat, add the lime
or lemon juice and mix well. Sprinkle
the Crispy Fried Shallots over it just
before serving.

Makes 1/2 cup (125 ml)
Preparation time: 20 mins
Cooking time: 25 mins

Sambal Soto
Chili Dip for Soto

3 candlenuts, deep-fried whole until
  golden
4–5 red finger-length chilies or 5–7
  bird's-eye chilies, deseeded
6 shallots, peeled
2–3 cloves garlic, peeled
1 teaspoon sugar
1/4 teaspoon salt
1/4 cup (60 ml) freshly squeezed lime
  or lemon juice

Grind the candlenuts, chilies, shallots
and garlic to a smooth paste in a
mortar or blender, adding a little

lime or lemon juice if necessary to
keep the mixture turning. Season
the ground paste with the sugar,
salt and lime or lemon juice. Serve
in a small bowl.

Makes 1 cup
Preparation time: 15 mins

Spiced Coconut with Peanuts   Serundeng

2 shallots, peeled
2 cloves garlic, peeled
2 teaspoons shaved palm sugar or
  dark brown sugar
1 teaspoon dried shrimp paste (*trasi*),
  dry-roasted (page 23)
1 tablespoon tamarind juice (page 26)
4 cups (400 g) freshly grated coconut
  or 3 cups (240 g) unsweetened desiccated coconut
2/3 cup (100 g) roasted unsalted
  peanuts, skins discarded
1/2 teaspoon salt

1 Grind the shallots, garlic, sugar,
shrimp paste and tamarind juice to
a smooth paste in a mortar or
blender. Add the grated coconut
and mix well.
2 Dry-fry the mixture in a wok or
skillet over very low heat for 10 to
15 minutes until golden brown and
flaky. Add the peanuts and salt, and
mix until well blended. Remove from
the heat and set aside to cool.
Serve in small bowls or sprinkle
over rice or side dishes. *Serundeng*
keeps for 2 weeks in an airtight
container.

Makes 3 cups
Preparation time: 15 mins
Cooking time: 15 mins

Classic Gado Gado   Tofu and Vegetable Salad with Peanut Dressing

1 cup (50 g) bean sprouts, seed coats and tails discarded
2 cups (180 g) spinach, rinsed, tough stems discarded
1 carrot, sliced
1 cup (100 g) green beans, cut into short lengths
1/4 head cabbage, leaves separated and sliced
2 cakes (about 7 oz/200 g each) deep-fried tofu, sliced
2 hard-boiled eggs, cut into wedges
2 tablespoons Crispy Fried Shallots (page 34), to garnish
Krupuk shrimp crackers (page 24), to serve (optional)

Gado Gado Dressing
1 cup (150 g) roasted unsalted peanuts
2 cloves garlic, peeled
2–3 bird's-eye chilies or red finger-length chilies, deseeded
1 in (2$^1/_2$ cm) fresh *kencur* root, peeled and sliced
1 kaffir lime leaf
3 tablespoons sweet Indonesian soy sauce (*kecap manis*)
1/2 teaspoon salt
2 cups (500 ml) water
1 teaspoon freshly squeezed lime or lemon juice

1 Prepare the Crispy Fried Shallots by following the recipe on page 34.
2 To make the Gado Gado Dressing, coarsely grind the peanuts, garlic, chilies and *kencur* in a mortar or blender, adding a little water if necessary to keep the mixture turning. Place the ground mixture in a saucepan with all the other Dressing ingredients, except the lime or lemon juice, and simmer uncovered over very low heat for about 1 hour, stirring frequently to prevent the sauce from sticking to the pot and burning. Remove from the heat and set aside. Add the lime or lemon juice, mix well and sprinkle 1 tablespoon of the Crispy Fried Shallots over the sauce just before serving.
3 Bring a saucepan of water to a boil over medium heat, and briefly blanch the vegetables (about 30 seconds for bean sprouts, 1 minute for spinach, 1 to 2 minutes for carrot, and 2 to 3 minutes for green beans and cabbage). Remove from the heat and drain.
4 Arrange all the vegetables on a serving platter and top with the tofu and egg wedges. Garnish with the remaining Crispy Fried Shallots and drizzle the Gado Gado Dressing on top. Serve with the deep-fried *krupuk* on the side.

Serves 4 to 6   Preparation time: 35 mins   Cooking time: 1 hour

Crispy Peanut Wafers   Rempeyek Kacang

1$^1/_2$ cups (220 g) raw peanuts
1 cup (120 g) rice flour
$^3/_4$ cup (100 g) flour
1 cup (250 ml) thick coconut milk
Oil, for deep-frying

Spice Paste
2 candlenuts, roughly chopped
1/2 in (1 cm) fresh turmeric, peeled and sliced, or 1/2 teaspoon ground turmeric
2 cloves garlic, peeled
1 teaspoon coriander seeds
2 kaffir lime leaves (optional)
1/2 teaspoon salt

1 Dry-roast the peanuts in a wok or skillet over low heat for about 5 minutes. Remove from the heat and set aside to cool, then rub the peanuts together to remove the skins.
2 To make the Spice Paste, grind all the ingredients to a smooth paste in a mortar or blender, adding a little coconut milk if necessary to keep the mixture turning. Combine the ground paste and flours in a mixing bowl, add the coconut milk and stir well to obtain a smooth batter, then add the peanuts and mix well.
3 Heat the oil in a wok over medium heat until hot. Ladle 2 tablespoons of the batter at a time into the hot oil and deep-fry until crispy and golden brown, 3 to 5 minutes. Remove from the wok and drain the wafer on paper towels. Continue to deep-fry the wafers until all the batter is used up. Allow the wafers to cool thoroughly before storing them in an airtight container.

Makes about 30 wafers   Preparation time: 20 mins   Cooking time: 25 mins

Fragrant Beef Satay   Sate Sapi

1½ lbs (700 g) top round beef
30 Bamboo skewers, soaked in water
   for 4 hours before using
2 portions Sambal Kacang (page 34)

Spice Paste
4 candlenuts, roughly chopped
2 in (5 cm) fresh galangal, peeled
   and sliced
1 in (2½ cm) fresh ginger, peeled
   and sliced
2–3 red finger-length chilies, deseeded
5 shallots, peeled
3 cloves garlic, peeled
½ teaspoon freshly ground black
   pepper
1 teaspoon coriander seeds or
   ground coriander
3 tablespoons shaved palm sugar
1 teaspoon salt
2 tablespoons oil
1 *salam* leaf

1 Prepare the Sambal Kacang by following the recipe on page 34.
2 Cut the beef into 1-in (2½-cm) cubes and set aside.
3 Make the Spice Paste by grinding all the ingredients, except the oil and *salam* leaf, to a smooth paste in a mortar or blender, adding a little oil if necessary to keep the mixture turning. Heat the oil in a wok over medium heat and stir-fry the ground paste with the *salam* leaf for 3 to 5 minutes until fragrant. Remove from the heat and set aside to cool.
4 When cooled, place the Spice Paste and beef in a large bowl and mix well. Set aside in the refrigerator to marinate overnight.
5 Soak the bamboo skewers in water for 4 hours before using so they do not burn when grilling the meat. Thread the marinated beef onto the skewers and grill over hot charcoal or under a preheated broiler for 2 to 3 minutes on each side, basting with the marinade, until cooked. Turn the skewers frequently to prevent the beef from burning, it should be browned on the outside and cooked on the inside.
6 Arrange the beef satay on a serving platter and serve with a bowl of Sambal Kecap or Sambal Kacang on the side.

Serves 6 to 8   Preparation time: 45 mins + to marinate overnight
Cooking time: 45 mins

Balinese Style Chicken or Duck Satay   Sate Lilit

1 lb (500 g) ground chicken or duck
2 cups (200 g) freshly grated coconut
3 kaffir lime leaves, thinly sliced
2 tablespoons shaved palm sugar
1 teaspoon salt
24 lemongrass or bamboo skewers
2 portions Sambal Kecap (page 33)

Spice Paste
2 candlenuts, roughly chopped
½ in (1 cm) fresh galangal, peeled
   and sliced
½ in (1 cm) fresh *kencur* root, peeled
   and sliced
½ in (1 cm) fresh turmeric, peeled
   and sliced, or 1 teaspoon ground
   turmeric
2 red finger-length chilies, deseeded
4–6 shallots, peeled
2 cloves garlic, peeled
¼ teaspoon ground cloves
2 teaspoons coriander seeds
½ teaspoon freshly ground black
   pepper or black peppercorns
Pinch of ground nutmeg
1 teaspoon dried shrimp paste (*trasi*),
   dry-roasted (page 23)
1 tablespoon oil

1 Prepare the Sambal Kecap by following the recipe on page 33.
2 Make the Spice Paste by grinding all the ingredients, except the oil, to a smooth paste in a mortar or blender, adding a little oil if necessary to keep the mixture turning. Heat the oil in a wok over medium heat and stir-fry the ground paste for 3 to 5 minutes, then remove from the heat and set aside to cool.
3 When cooled, mix the Spice Paste with the ground chicken or duck and all the other ingredients, except the skewers, until well blended. Set aside to marinate for 2 hours in the refrigerator.
4 If using bamboo skewers, soak them in water for 4 hours before using. Mold about 2 heaped tablespoons of the meat mixture onto each lemongrass or bamboo skewer with your hands and press it together firmly to form a kebab. Repeat until all the meat mixture is used up.
5 Grill the skewers over hot charcoal or under a preheated broiler for 2 to 3 minutes on each side, basting with the marinade, until cooked. Turn the skewers frequently to prevent the meat from burning. Arrange the satay on a serving platter and serve hot with the Sambal Kecap.

Serves 4 to 6   Preparation time: 45 mins + 2 hours to marinate
Cooking time: 20 mins

Lotek   Steamed Vegetables with Peanut Dressing

The sauce served with this cooked vegetable salad has ground peanuts for extra flavor and nutrition. It is said that Sundanese women have such beautiful skin because they eat so many vegetables.

6 oz (175 g) water spinach (*kangkung*)
  or spinach
6 oz (175 g) pumpkin or squash
6 oz (175 g) green beans
1 large potato, peeled and diced
1 cup (50 g) bean sprouts, seed coats
  and tails discarded

Lotek Dressing
$1/2$ cup (75 g) fried or roasted unsalted
  peanuts
$3/4$ in (2 cm) fresh *kencur* root, peeled
  and sliced
2–3 bird's-eye chilies, deseeded
$1/2$ teaspoon dried shrimp paste
  (*trasi*), dry-roasted (page 23)
1 teaspoon shaved palm sugar or
  dark brown sugar
1 teaspoon salt
2 tablespoons water

1 Make the Lotek Dressing by pulsing the peanuts in a blender until coarsely ground, then add the *kencur*, chilies, dried shrimp paste, palm sugar, salt and water and grind to a smooth sauce. Set aside.
2 To prepare the vegetables, rinse and trim the young shoots of the water spinach or spinach from the main stems. Peel and dice the pumpkin or squash. Cut the green beans into lengths. Bring a saucepan of water to a boil over medium heat, then blanch the vegetables until cooked (about 30 seconds for the bean sprouts, 1 minute for the spinach, 1 to 2 minutes for the pumpkin and potato, and 2 to 3 minutes for the green beans). Drain and place the blanched vegetables on a serving platter.
3 Drizzle the dressing over the vegetables, then toss well to coat the vegetables before serving.

Serves 4   Preparation time: 20 mins   Cooking time: 5 mins

Karedok   Raw Vegetable Salad with Palm Sugar Dressing

The Sundanese of West Java are renowned for their love of vegetables, both raw and cooked, and often eat them as between-meal snacks. Serve Karedok with rice as part of a main meal.

$1/4$ head round cabbage
1 small cucumber
2 cups (100 g) bean sprouts, seed
  coats and tails discarded
1 slender Asian eggplant, thinly sliced
1 cup (100 g) thinly sliced green beans
2 tablespoons Crispy Fried Shallots
  (page 34), to garnish
Krupuk shrimp crackers (page 24),
  to serve

Karedok Dressing
1 in ($2^1/2$ cm) fresh *kencur* root,
  peeled and sliced
3–4 red finger-length chilies, deseeded
3 cloves garlic, peeled
3 tablespoons shaved palm sugar
  or dark brown sugar
$1/2$ teaspoon dried shrimp paste
  (*trasi*), dry-roasted (page 23)
2 tablespoons tamarind juice (page 26)
2 tablespoons warm water
1 teaspoon salt

1 Prepare the Crispy Fried Shallots by following the recipe on page 34.
2 To make the Karedok Dressing, grind all the ingredients to a smooth paste in a mortar or blender. Set aside.
3 Separate the cabbage leaves, rinse well and shake dry, then slice them very thinly and place in a large bowl. Peel the cucumber, quarter it lengthwise and slice the quarters across very thinly. Place in the bowl with the cabbage. Rinse and drain the bean sprouts and place in the bowl. Add the eggplant and green beans.
4 Pour the Dressing over the vegetables and toss well. Garnish with Crispy Fried Shallots and serve with *krupuk*.

Serves 4   Preparation time: 25 mins

Marinated Shrimp

Belimbing wuluh are small, sour carambola fruits which grow abundantly in house gardens throughout Indonesia and other parts of Southeast Asia. They add a delicious tang to this North Sumatran salad, although tamarind may also be used instead.

1½ lbs (700 g) large fresh shrimp
4 cups (1 liter) water
2 red finger-length chilies, deseeded
4 shallots, peeled
2 *belimbing wuluh* (carambola), or 2 tablespoons tamarind juice (page 26)
Sprigs of fresh parsley or coriander leaves (cilantro), to garnish
Bottled sweet chili sauce, to serve

1 Bring the shrimp and water to a boil in a large saucepan. Immediately reduce the heat and simmer until the shrimp turn pink, 2 to 3 minutes. Quickly drain and plunge the shrimp into a basin of iced water for 30 seconds to stop the cooking. Drain, peel and devein the shrimp. Transfer to a serving platter and set aside.
2 Grind the chilies, shallots and *belimbing* or tamarind juice to a smooth paste in a mortar or blender, adding a little lime or lemon juice for a more sour taste if desired. Set aside.
3 Add the ground paste to the shrimp and toss gently until well coated. Garnish with parsley or coriander leaves (cilantro), and serve with a small bowl of sweet chili sauce on the side.

Serves 4 to 6   Preparation time: 20 mins   Cooking time: 5 mins

Fresh Tuna and Green Mango Salad   Sambal Tappa

This recipe comes from Ambon, Maluku, where fresh tuna is abundant. If fresh tuna is not available, use canned tuna as a substitute, although the flavor is not the same.

1 to 2 unripe mangoes (1 lb/500 g in total), peeled and pitted, then thinly sliced into matchsticks
1 teaspoon salt
1 lb (500 g) fresh tuna steaks, grilled and deboned, flesh flaked
3 to 4 shallots, peeled and sliced
1 teaspoon ground white pepper
3 tablespoons thick coconut milk

1 Place the mango shreds in a colander. Sprinkle the salt over them and mix well. Set aside to drain for 10 minutes, then squeeze the mango to remove as much liquid as possible.
2 Place the mango in a large salad bowl. Add the flaked tuna, shallots, pepper and coconut milk, and toss well. Serve chilled.

Serves 4 to 6   Preparation time: 25 mins

Seasoned Fish Grilled in Banana Leaves   Pepes Ikan

This Kalimantan recipe calls for steamed bundles of flaky, seasoned fish to be grilled directly over hot charcoal, giving an inimitable flavor.

1 lb (500 g) white fish fillets, skinned and cut into chunks
4–5 shallots, peeled
3 cloves garlic, peeled
2 spring onions, sliced
1 teaspoon ground white pepper
$1/_3$ cup (85 ml) thick coconut milk
1 tablespoon freshly squeezed lime or lemon juice
$1/_2$ teaspoon salt
2 eggs
Banana leaves or aluminum foil, cut into 8-in (20-cm) square pieces, for wrapping

1 Place the fish chunks in a blender or food processor and pulse for a few seconds, then add all the other ingredients, except the banana leaves, and grind to a thick paste. Set aside.
2 Scald the banana leaves by pouring boiling water over them in a basin, so they become flexible. Drain and place the leaves on a clean work surface. Spoon 3 heaped tablespoons of the fish mixture onto each piece of banana leaf (or aluminum foil) and wrap it up as directed for *pepes* on page 19. Repeat until all the fish mixture is used up.
3 Grill each parcel directly over hot charcoal or under a preheated broiler for 10 to 15 minutes, turning from time to time until the banana leaf wrapper is charred. Serve hot.

Serves 4 to 6   Preparation time: 40 mins   Cooking time: 30 mins

Fragrant Fried Fish Cakes   Otak Otak Pipih

These Javanese fish cakes are flavored with coconut, spices and shallots, and can be prepared several hours in advance and kept refrigerated before the final deep-frying.

1 cup (100 g) freshly grated coconut or 1 cup (80 g) unsweetened desiccated coconut
1 lb (500 g) white fish fillets, skinned and cut into chunks
2 eggs
1 teaspoon sugar
1 teaspoon salt
1 cup (250 ml) thick coconut milk
Oil, for deep-frying
1 portion Pickled Shallots (page 32), to serve
$1/_2$ portion Sambal Soto (page 34), to serve

Spice Paste
2 candlenuts, roughly chopped
$1/_2$ in (1 cm) fresh galangal, peeled and sliced
$1/_2$ in (1 cm) fresh ginger, peeled and sliced
3 shallots, peeled
2 cloves garlic, peeled

1 Prepare the Pickled Shallots and Sambal Soto by following the recipes on pages 32 and 34.
2 Dry-fry the grated coconut in a skillet over low heat, stirring constantly until golden brown, about 10 minutes for fresh coconut and 5 to 7 minutes for desiccated coconut. Do not allow the coconut to burn. Set aside to cool in a small bowl.
3 Make the Spice Paste by grinding all the ingredients in a mortar or blender, adding a little oil if necessary to keep the mixture turning. Add the fish chunks and grind until fine.
4 Place the ground mixture in a large bowl. Add the eggs, sugar and salt, and mix well. Shape the mixture into small balls, then flatten with your palm and shape them into patties.
5 Heat the oil in a wok and deep-fry the patties until cooked and golden brown on all sides, 3 to 5 minutes. Remove from the oil and drain on paper towels. Serve hot with serving bowls of the Pickled Shallots and Sambal Soto on the side.

Serves 4 to 6   Preparation time: 20 mins + time to prepare the pickles and sambal
Cooking time: 25 mins + time to prepare the pickles and sambal

Martabak   Pancakes with Curried Meat Filling

This Indian Muslim speciality, a night-time favorite, is often bought as a snack or light meal from food stalls.

2 tablespoons oil
4 cloves garlic, minced
12 oz (350 g) ground lamb or beef
1 onion, diced
1 small leek, halved lengthwise and very thinly sliced
1 red finger-length chili, deseeded and sliced
3 tablespoons minced celery leaves
1 tablespoon curry powder
4 eggs
1 spring onion, thinly sliced
$1/2$ teaspoon salt
$1/2$ teaspoon ground white pepper
Green chilies, deseeded, to serve (optional)
1 portion Mixed Vegetable Pickles (page 31), to serve

Dough
2 cups (300 g) flour
3 tablespoons oil
$3/4$ cup (185 ml) water
$1/2$ teaspoon salt

1 Prepare the Mixed Vegetable Pickles by following the recipe on page 31.
2 Make the Dough by combining and kneading all the ingredients to form an oily, elastic dough. Cover and set aside at room temperature for 2 hours, then quarter the Dough and roll each piece into a ball. Lightly oil a rolling pin and roll out the Dough on an oiled smooth surface to make a large thin circle. Repeat with the rest of the Dough and set aside.
3 To prepare the filling, heat the oil in a wok or skillet over high heat and stir-fry the garlic for a few seconds until fragrant and golden brown. Add the ground meat and stir-fry until it changes color, about 2 minutes. Add the onion, leek, chili and celery leaves, and stir-fry for 2 more minutes. Add the curry powder and stir-fry until well blended, 2 to 3 minutes. Remove from the heat and set aside to cool. Divide the cooked filling into 4 equal portions. Add 1 egg, a little spring onion, salt and pepper to each portion and mix well.
4 Heat a heavy griddle or skillet over medium heat until hot. Place 1 portion of the filling onto the center of each Dough, then fold over the sides of the Dough to completely enclose the filling and form a package. Place the package on the hot griddle or skillet and pan-fry until golden brown, 2 to 3 minutes, then flip it over and fry the other side until browned. Repeat with the rest of the Dough and filling.
5 Serve hot with fresh green chilies (if using) and a bowl of the Mixed Vegetable Pickles on the side. For a more elaborate presentation, garnish with spring onions, chilies and celery leaves.

Makes 4 Martabak   Preparation time: 30 mins + time to prepare the pickles
Cooking time: 25 mins

Rujak   Fruit and Vegetable Salad with Sweet Tamarind Dressing

This popular snack, an intriguing mixture of sweet, sour and spicy flavors, is prepared at countless *warungs* throughout Indonesia. The list of raw fruits and vegetables that can be included is endless—and simply depends on what is available and what you feel like eating.

$^{1}/_{2}$ small pineapple, peeled, eyes and fibrous core discarded, then sliced

1 unripe mango, peeled and pitted, flesh sliced

1 small cucumber, peeled, deseeded and sliced

3 water apples (see note) or 1 green apple, rinsed and sliced

1 starfruit, sliced

$^{1}/_{2}$ small papaya, peeled, halved, deseeded and sliced

1 portion Sambal Rujak (page 34)

1 Prepare the Sambal Rujak by following the recipe on page 34.
2 Place all the cut fruits and vegetables in a large salad bowl, drizzle the Sambal Rujak over them and toss to coat well. Serve immediately.

Note: Although this is served as a snack in Indonesia, you can serve it as an appetizer or as part of a meal or buffet. **Water apples** (*jambu air*) are very juicy and crunchy fruits that come in three colors: red, white and pink. They have a mild flavor and crisp texture. They have a thin, edible skin which looks a little waxy.

Serves 6 to 8   Preparation time: 45 mins   Cooking time: 20 mins

Nasi Kebuli   Seasoned Rice with Chicken and Pineapple

1 lb (500 g) boneless chicken, diced
3 cups (750 ml) chicken stock or 1$^1/_2$
   teaspoons chicken stock granules
   dissolved in 3 cups (750 ml) warm
   water
1 teaspoon salt
2 cups (400 g) uncooked rice, washed
$^1/_2$ small pineapple (about 8 oz/250 g)
Crispy Fried Shallots (page 34),
   to garnish

Rice Seasonings
2 tablespoons butter or oil
6 shallots, peeled and sliced
5 cloves garlic, peeled and sliced
3 cardamom pods, bruised
2 cloves
1 stalk lemongrass, thick bottom third
   only, outer layers discarded, inner
   part bruised
1 in (2$^1/_2$ cm) fresh ginger, peeled
   and thinly sliced
1 cinnamon stick
1 teaspoon coriander seeds
$^1/_2$ teaspoon white peppercorns

1 Prepare the Crispy Fried Shallots by following the recipe on page 34.
2 To make the Rice Seasonings, heat the butter or oil in a wok over high heat and stir-fry all the ingredients until fragrant, 2 to 3 minutes.
3 Add the chicken to the wok and stir-fry for 2 to 3 minutes. Pour in the chicken stock, mix well and season with the salt, then bring the ingredients to a boil. Reduce the heat to medium and simmer uncovered until the chicken is tender, about 5 minutes. Remove from the heat. Strain and reserve the stock. Set the chicken pieces aside and discard all the other solids.
4 Bring the uncooked rice and 2$^1/_2$ cups (625 ml) of the reserved stock to a boil over high heat in a pot. Reduce the heat to medium, cover and simmer until the rice is almost cooked and the liquid is absorbed, 5 to 10 minutes. Add the chicken, mix well and continue to simmer uncovered until the rice is fluffy, 5 to 10 minutes, then remove from the heat. Alternatively, cook the rice in a rice cooker with 2$^1/_2$ cups (625 ml) of the reserved stock and add the chicken during the last 5 minutes of cooking.
5 Peel the pineapple, rinse, remove the eyes and fibrous core, and diced. Transfer the cooled rice to a serving platter, garnish with the pineapple and Crispy Fried Shallots, and serve hot.

Serves 6 to 8   Preparation time: 30 mins   Cooking time: 35 mins

Classic Nasi Goreng   Indonesian Fried Rice

One of Indonesia's most popular dishes, Nasi Goreng is prepared in countless ways and is eaten morning, noon and night. This classic version is accompanied by fried egg, fried chicken, satay and *krupuk* (deep-fried shrimp crackers) for a substantial meal. Any sort of leftover or fresh meat or shrimp may be added, but the true flavor of Indonesia comes from the use of pungent chilies and *trasi* (dried shrimp paste).

5 cups (500 g) cold cooked rice or leftover rice
3 tablespoons oil
4 eggs
4–5 shallots, peeled and sliced
2 cloves garlic, peeled and sliced
1–2 red finger-length chilies, deseeded and minced
2 teaspoons dried shrimp paste (*trasi*), dry-roasted (page 23)
5 oz (150 g) fresh shrimp, peeled and deveined
1 cup (200 g) leftover cooked chicken, lamb or beef, diced
2 cups (250 g) thinly sliced cabbage
1 teaspoon salt
1 tablespoon sweet Indonesian soy sauce (*kecap manis*)
Sliced cucumber and sliced tomato, to garnish (optional)

Accompaniments
1 portion Javanese Fried Chicken (page 67)
1/2 portion Beef Satay (page 38)
Crispy Fried Shallots (page 34)
1 portion Sambal Kecap (page 33)
Krupuk shrimp crackers (page 24)
1/2 portion Mixed Vegetable Pickles (page 31)

1 Prepare the Javanese Fried Chicken, Beef Satay, Crispy Fried Shallots, Sambal Kecap and Mixed Vegetable Pickles by following the respective recipes.
2 Flake the cold rice with a fork or your fingers to separate the grains. Set aside.
3 Lightly grease a non-stick skillet with a little oil and fry the eggs sunny side up. Remove from the heat and set aside.
4 Heat the remaining oil in a wok over medium heat and stir-fry the shallots, garlic, minced chili and dried shrimp paste until fragrant, 1 to 2 minutes. Add the shrimp and stir-fry until almost cooked, about 2 minutes, then add the cabbage and leftover cooked meat, and continue to stir-fry until the cabbage is slightly wilted, about 2 minutes. Increase the heat to high, add the rice, salt and sweet Indonesian soy sauce, and stir-fry briskly until all the ingredients are mixed well and heated through, about 2 minutes. Remove from the heat.
5 Transfer the fried rice to a serving platter, top with the fried eggs and arrange the fried chicken and satays on the side. Garnish with cucumber and tomato slices (if using) and serve with the Accompaniments on the side.

Note: It is essential to use cold rice for this dish. Freshly cooked rice is too soft and will absorb the oil, resulting in an oily and mushy fried rice. In Asia, leftover rice is used the next day for any fried rice dish as it is easier to fry.

Serves 4   Preparation time: 30 mins + time to prepare the Accompaniments
Cooking time: 15 mins + time to prepare the Accompaniments

Soto Ayam with Potato Croquettes   Chicken Noodle Soup

Soto is a robust soup made with lemongrass, turmeric and coriander, and served with noodles, *lontong* (compressed rice) or potato croquettes (*pergedel*). If desired, the croquettes can be omitted and the dish can be garnished with potato chips or *emping* (melinjo nut wafers, see photo).

1 fresh chicken
12 cups (3 liters) water
2 stalks lemongrass, thick bottom
   third only, outer layers discarded,
   inner part bruised
3 kaffir lime leaves
2 sprigs Chinese celery leaves, sliced
1$^1/_2$ teaspoons salt
$^1/_2$ teaspoon ground white pepper
7 oz (200 g) dried glass noodles
   (*tanghoon*), soaked in water to soften
   (see note), or dried rice vermicelli
   (*beehoon*)
5 hard-boiled eggs, peeled and
   quartered
1 cup (50 g) bean sprouts, seed
   coats and tails discarded, rinsed
   and blanched in hot water
Crispy Fried Shallots (page 34),
   to garnish
2 tablespoons sliced Chinese celery
   leaves, to garnish
Lime wedges, to serve
1 portion Sambal Soto (page 34)

Potato Croquettes
2 potatoes, boiled, peeled and
   mashed
$^1/_4$ teaspoon ground white pepper
1 spring onion, thinly sliced
$^1/_4$ teaspoon salt
$^1/_4$ teaspoon freshly grated nutmeg
   or ground nutmeg
1 tablespoon minced celery leaves
2 tablespoons Crispy Fried Shallots
   (page 34)
Oil, for deep-frying
1 egg, beaten

Spice Paste
1 in (2$^1/_2$ cm) fresh turmeric, peeled
   and sliced, or 1 teaspoon ground
   turmeric
5 shallots, peeled
5 cloves garlic, peeled
2 tablespoons ground coriander
1 tablespoon oil

1 Prepare the Sambal Soto by following the recipe on page 34.
2 Clean and rinse the chicken well. Bring the water to a boil over high heat in a large pot, then immerse the chicken into the boiling water and boil for 15 minutes. Turn off the heat and leave the chicken to steep in the pot for 15 to 20 minutes. Remove and drain the chicken. Strain and reserve the stock. Separate the chicken meat from the bone and tear the meat into thin shreds. Set aside.
3 Make the Potato Croquettes by combining the mashed potato with all the other ingredients, except the oil and egg, and mixing well. Shape the mixture into patties and set aside to chill in the refrigerator for 45 minutes. Heat the oil in a wok over medium heat. Dip each patty in the beaten egg, then lower it into the hot oil and deep-fry until golden brown, 2 to 3 minutes on each side. Remove from the heat and drain on paper towels. Repeat until all the patties are cooked.
4 To make the Spice Paste, grind the turmeric, shallots, garlic and coriander to a smooth paste in a mortar or blender, adding a little oil if necessary to keep the mixture turning. Heat the oil in a wok or skillet over medium heat and stir-fry the ground paste until fragrant, 3 to 5 minutes. Set aside.
5 Bring 8 cups (2 liters) of the reserved chicken stock, lemongrass, kaffir lime leaves and celery leaves to a boil in a pot. Reduce the heat to low and simmer uncovered for about 15 minutes. Season with the salt and pepper, and keep the broth hot over very low heat.
6 To serve, portion the softened glass noodles and shredded chicken into individual serving bowls. Ladle the hot broth over and top with hard-boiled eggs, bean sprouts and Potato Croquettes. Garnish with Crispy Fried Shallots and celery leaves, and serve with lime wedges and a bowl of the Sambal Soto on the side.

Note: Dried glass noodles (*tanghoon*), made from mung bean flour, are also called transparent or cellophane noodles. They are used in soups and vegetable dishes. Substitute dried rice vermicelli—see package instructions for preparation. To save time, prepare the chicken stock and Potato Croquettes in advance and reheat just before serving.

Serves 6 to 8   Preparation time: 1 hour + 45 mins chilling
Cooking time: 55 mins

Festive Turmeric Rice   Nasi Kuning

Rice colored with turmeric and shaped into a cone is a common sight during festive occasions in Bali and Java. The conical shape echoes that of the mythical Hindu mountain, Meru, while yellow is the color of royalty and one of the four sacred colors for Hindus. Even on Muslim Java, this traditional festive dish remains popular, and is accompanied by Sambal Trasi (page 33), Classic Grilled Chicken (page 64) and Eggs in Fragrant Lemongrass Sauce (page 76).

2 in (5 cm) fresh turmeric, peeled and sliced, or 2 teaspoons ground turmeric
$1/4$ cup (60 ml) water
$1^1/_2$ cups (300 g) uncooked rice, washed and drained
$1^1/_2$ cups (375 ml) thin coconut milk
$1/_2$ cup (125 ml) chicken stock or $1/_4$ teaspoon chicken stock granules
  dissolved in $1/_2$ cup (125 ml) warm water
1 *salam* or pandanus leaf
1 stalk lemongrass, thick bottom third only, outer layers discarded,
  inner part bruised
1 in ($2^1/_2$ cm) fresh galangal, peeled and sliced
1 teaspoon salt

Accompaniments
Freshly sliced cucumber and tomato
1 portion Sambal Trasi (page 33)
1 portion Grilled Chicken (page 64)
1 portion Sambal Goreng Tempeh (page 60)
1 portion Eggs in Fragrant Lemongrass Sauce (page 76)
Emping (melinjo nut wafers)

1 Prepare the Accompaniments by following the respective recipes.
2 Grind the turmeric and water in a mortar until fine. Strain through a sieve to extract all the juice. Discard the solids. If using ground turmeric, dissolve the powder in 2 tablespoons of water.
3 Combine the rice, turmeric juice, coconut milk, chicken stock, *salam* or pandanus leaf, lemongrass, galangal and salt in a pot and bring to a boil over high heat. Reduce the heat to medium and simmer covered until the liquid is absorbed, 10 to 15 minutes, then reduce the heat to low and cook for 5 to 10 more minutes, until the rice is dry and fluffy. Remove from the heat and mix well. Alternatively, cook the rice and ingredients in a rice cooker.
4 Discard the *salam* or pandanus leaf, lemongrass and galangal. Press the cooked turmeric rice into a cone shape, if desired. Serve the cooked rice with the Accompaniments on the side.

Serves 4 to 6   Preparation time: 15 mins + time to prepare the Accompaniments
Cooking time: 15 mins + time to prepare the Accompaniments

Sayur Asam   Vegetables in Sweet Tamarind Broth

4 cups (1 liter) water
2 *salam* leaves (optional)
1 in (2$^1/_2$ cm) fresh galangal, bruised
1 fresh or frozen corn cob, cut into
  sections
2 cups (180 g) tapioca leaves, sweet
  potato leaves, spinach and *melinjo*
  leaves (see note)
1 cup (100 g) green beans, cut into
  short lengths
2 to 3 green finger-length chilies,
  deseeded and cut into short lengths
  (optional)
$^1/_2$ cup (75 g) lightly boiled raw
  peanuts or fresh *melinjo* nuts
$^1/_4$ cup (60 ml) tamarind juice
  (page 26) or 4 to 6 carambola
  (*belimbing wuluh*), sliced
$^1/_2$ cup (125 g) small fresh shrimp,
  peeled and deveined (optional)
1 ripe tomato, cut into wedges
2 tablespoons sugar
$^1/_2$ teaspoon salt

Spice Paste
2 to 4 finger-length chilies, deseeded
4 shallots, peeled
3 cloves garlic, peeled
$^1/_2$ teaspoon salt

1 Make the Spice Paste by grinding all the ingredients to a smooth paste in a mortar or blender, adding a little water if necessary to keep the mixture turning. Set aside.
2 Bring the water to a boil over medium heat in a large saucepan. Add the Spice Paste, *salam* leaves (if using) and galangal, mix well and bring to a boil again, then simmer uncovered for 2 minutes. Add the corn and boil for 2 more minutes, then add the vegetables, chili (if using), peanuts and tamarind juice or carambola. Bring the mixture to a boil and simmer until the vegetables are tender, 3 to 5 minutes. Finally add the shrimp, tomato and sugar, and simmer for 1 to 2 minutes until the shrimp turn pink. Season with the salt and remove from the heat. Serve hot as part of a rice-based meal.

Note: In Asia, the tender leaves of many vegetable plants are cooked as vegetables. Tapioca leaves, sweet potato leaves and *melinjo* leaves are readily available in Indonesia. Substitute water spinach (*kangkung*), or regular spinach or bok choy.

Serves 4 to 6   Preparation time: 30 mins   Cooking time: 20 mins

Water Spinach with Coconut and Spicy Dressing   Pelecing Kangkung

10 oz (300 g) water spinach
  (*kangkung*) or regular spinach
1 kaffir lime leaf
1 clove garlic, peeled
1 teaspoon shaved palm sugar or
  dark brown sugar
1 cup (100 g) freshly grated coconut
3 bird's-eye chilies or red finger-
  length chilies, deseeded
$^1/_2$ teaspoon dried shrimp paste
  (*trasi*), dry-roasted (page 23)
1 teaspoon salt
1 teaspoon freshly squeezed lime or
  lemon juice
2 tablespoons warm water
2 tablespoons roasted unsalted
  peanuts
4 limes, halved, to serve

1 Wash the spinach well and discard the tough stems. Cut into lengths. Blanch in boiling water for 1 to 2 minutes, then set aside on a plate.
2 Grind the kaffir lime leaf, garlic, palm sugar and grated coconut in a blender until fine and set aside in a bowl, then grind the chilies, dried shrimp paste, salt, lime or lemon juice and water to a smooth paste.
3 To serve, toss the blanched spinach with the dried shrimp paste mixture. Sprinkle the grated coconut mixture and peanuts on top and serve with lime halves on the side.

Note: If water spinach is not available, substitute any other leafy green vegetable such as spinach or Chinese cabbage.

Serves 4   Preparation time: 20 mins   Cooking time: 2 mins

Stewed Pineapple with Coconut and Indonesian Spices   Gulai Nanas

1 large ripe pineapple (2 lbs/1 kg)
2 tablespoons oil
$3^1/_2$ cups (875 ml) thin coconut milk
$1/_4$ teaspoon freshly ground black
  pepper
2 star anise pods
1 cinnamon stick
2 cloves
$1/_4$ teaspoon ground nutmeg
1 stalk lemongrass, thick bottom
  third only, outer layers discarded,
  inner part bruised
1 in ($2^1/_2$ cm) fresh galangal, peeled
  and sliced
1 tablespoon tamarind juice (page 26)
$1/_2$ teaspoon salt
$1/_2$ cup (125 ml) thick coconut milk
1 tablespoon Crispy Fried Shallots
  (page 34)

Spice Paste
2 candlenuts, roughly chopped
1 teaspoon coriander seeds or $1/_2$
  teaspoon ground coriander
$1/_2$ in (1 cm) fresh turmeric, peeled
  and sliced, or $1/_2$ teaspoon ground
  turmeric
3–4 dried red chilies, cut into lengths
  and soaked to soften
6 shallots, peeled
2 cloves garlic, peeled
1 teaspoon shaved palm sugar
  or dark brown sugar

Serves 4 to 6
Preparation time: 40 mins
Cooking time: 30 mins

1 Prepare the Crispy Fried Shallots by following the recipe on page 34.
2 Peel and core the pineapple and slice it into bite-sized chunks. Set aside.
3 Make the Spice Paste by grinding all the ingredients to a smooth paste in a mortar or blender, adding a little oil if necessary to keep the mixture turning.
4 Heat the oil in a wok over medium heat and stir-fry the Spice Paste until fragrant, 3 to 5 minutes. Add the thin coconut milk, stir gently and bring to a boil, Add the pineapple and all the other ingredients, except the thick coconut milk and Crispy Fried Shallots, and bring to a boil again. Reduce the heat to low and simmer covered until the pineapple is tender, 10 to 15 minutes. Add the thick coconut milk, stir well and allow it to heat through. Adjust the seasoning with more sugar or salt as desired and turn off the heat.
5 Transfer to a serving bowl, and garnish with Crispy Fried Shallots.

Vegetables with Spicy Coconut Sauce

7 oz (200 g) green beans, cut into
  lengths
2 cups (180 g) spinach leaves or
  young fern tips (fiddleheads)
1 cup (50 g) bean sprouts, seed
  coats and tails discarded
Crispy Fried Shallots (page 34)

Coconut Sauce
$1/_2$ in (1 cm) fresh turmeric, sliced, or
  1 teaspoon ground turmeric
2–3 bird's-eye chilies or red finger-
  length chilies, deseeded
2–3 shallots, peeled
2 cloves garlic, peeled
1 teaspoon shaved palm sugar
  or dark brown sugar
1 teaspoon dried shrimp paste
  (*trasi*), dry-roasted (page 23)
1 cup (100 g) freshly grated coconut
  or unsweetened desiccated coconut
1 cup (250 ml) water
1 *salam* leaf or bay leaf
$1/_4$ teaspoon salt

1 Prepare the Crispy Fried Shallots by following the recipe on page 34.
2 Make the Coconut Sauce by grinding the turmeric, chilies, shallots, garlic, palm sugar and shrimp paste to a smooth paste in a mortar or blender, adding a little water if necessary to keep the mixture turning. Place the ground paste with all the other ingredients in a saucepan and simmer uncovered over medium low heat for 5 to 10 minutes until the sauce thickens. Remove from the heat and set aside to cool.
3 Bring a saucepan of water to a boil over medium heat. Blanch the vegetables for 1 to 2 minutes. Remove from the heat, drain well and arrange on a serving platter.
4 Drizzle the Coconut Sauce over the vegetables and serve garnished with Crispy Fried Shallots or serve the sauce on the side as shown.

Serves 4   Preparation time: 25 mins   Cooking time: 15 mins

Sambal Goreng Tempeh   Sweet and Spicy Fried Tempeh

Sweetened with palm sugar and spiced with galangal, lemongrass, shrimp paste, tamarind and chilies, this dish is a Javanese favorite.

2 cakes tempeh (1 lb/500 g in total)
Oil, for deep-frying
2 shallots, peeled and sliced
3 cloves garlic, peeled and sliced
2 red finger-length chilies, deseeded and thinly sliced
1 in (2$^1/_2$ cm) fresh galangal, peeled and sliced
2 stalks lemongrass, thick bottom third only, outer layers discarded, inner part bruised
$^1/_2$ teaspoon dried shrimp paste (*trasi*), dry-roasted (page 23)
3 tablespoons shaved palm sugar or dark brown sugar
3 tablespoons water
2 tablespoons tamarind juice (page 26)
$^1/_2$ teaspoon salt

1 Slice the tempeh into long, narrow strips. Heat the oil in a wok over high heat and deep-fry the tempeh strips until browned and crispy, 3 to 5 minutes. Remove from the hot oil and set aside to drain on paper towels.
2 Drain the oil from the wok and wipe it clean. Heat 1 tablespoon of fresh oil in the wok over medium heat and stir-fry the shallots, garlic, chilies, galangal, lemongrass and dried shrimp paste for 3 to 5 minutes until fragrant. Add the palm sugar, water and tamarind juice, and stir-fry until the sugar has completely dissolved and begins to caramelize. Add the deep-fried tempeh strips and stir-fry until the sauce has thickened and completely coats the tempeh, 3 to 5 minutes. Season with the salt and remove from the heat. Discard the galangal and lemongrass, and garnish with sliced chili, if desired.

Serves 2 to 4   Preparation time: 20 mins   Cooking time: 20 mins

Tempeh Stewed in Coconut Milk and Spices   Gulai Tempeh

A Sumatran dish using protein-rich tempeh stewed with vegetables in a rich coconut gravy.

2 cups (500 ml) thick coconut milk
2 cloves
4 cakes tempeh (2 lbs/1 kg in total), cubed
8 oz (250 g) tapioca leaves, spinach or water spinach (*kangkung*)
$^1/_2$ teaspoon salt
1 spring onion, thinly sliced, to garnish
1 to 2 red finger-length chilies, deseeded and diced, to garnish

Spice Paste
1 teaspoon white peppercorns
1$^1/_2$ in (4 cm) fresh turmeric, peeled and sliced, or 1$^1/_2$ teaspoons ground turmeric
1 in (2$^1/_2$ cm) fresh ginger, peeled and sliced
4 cloves garlic, peeled
1 tablespoon shaved palm sugar or dark brown sugar

1 Make the Spice Paste by grinding all the ingredients to a smooth paste in a mortar or blender, adding a little coconut milk if necessary to keep the mixture turning.
2 Bring the coconut milk to a boil in a saucepan. Add the Spice Paste, cloves, tempeh and tapioca leaves or spinach and bring to a boil again. Reduce the heat to low and simmer uncovered, until the vegetables are tender and the sauce has thickened, 7 to 10 minutes. Season with the salt and garnish with freshly sliced spring onion and chili.

Serves 4 to 6   Preparation time: 20 mins   Cooking time: 15 mins

Fern Tips or Asparagus in Coconut Gravy   Gulai Daun Pakis

The young tips of several varieties of wild ferns are enjoyed in many parts of Indonesia. They are sold in wet markets throughout Southeast Asia and have an excellent flavor. Young asparagus or spinach make excellent substitutes.

2 cups (500 ml) thin coconut milk
1 lb (500 g) fresh fern tips (fiddleheads) or young asparagus, washed
2 *salam* leaves (optional)
1 tablespoon tamarind juice (page 26)
$1/2$ teaspoon salt

Spice Paste
1 in ($2^1/_2$ cm) fresh galangal, peeled
   and sliced
$1/2$ in (1 cm) fresh turmeric, peeled
   and sliced, or $1/2$ teaspoon ground
   turmeric
1 in ($2^1/_2$ cm) fresh ginger, peeled
   and sliced
2–3 red finger-length chilies,
   deseeded
3 shallots, peeled
2 cloves garlic, peeled

1 Make the Spice Paste by grinding all the ingredients to a smooth paste in a mortar or blender, adding a little coconut milk if necessary to keep the mixture turning.
2 Bring the Spice Paste and coconut milk to a boil in a saucepan. Reduce the heat to medium and simmer uncovered for 2 minutes. Add the fern tips or asparagus, *salam* leaves and tamarind juice, mix well and bring to a boil again, then simmer for about 15 minutes, stirring frequently until the vegetables are tender. Season with the salt and remove from the heat.
3 Transfer to a serving casserole and serve immediately with steamed rice.

Serves 4 to 6   Preparation time: 20 mins   Cooking time: 20 mins

Eggplant in Tamarind Broth   Asam Terong

A simple and quick vegetable dish that enhances the taste of eggplants.

2–3 red finger-length chilies, deseeded
   and sliced
3 shallots, sliced
2 cloves garlic, sliced
2 cups (500 ml) water
2–3 slender eggplants (1 lb/500 g),
   halved lengthwise and sliced
2 tablespoons tamarind juice (page
   26)
1 ripe tomato, cut into wedges
2 teaspoons shaved palm sugar
   or dark brown sugar
$1/2$ teaspoon salt

Garnishes
Crispy Fried Shallots (page 34)
2 tablespoons sliced Chinese celery
   leaves
1 spring onion, sliced

1 Prepare the Crispy Fried Shallots by following the recipe on page 34.
2 In a large saucepan, bring the sliced chili, shallot, garlic and water to a boil over medium heat, then simmer uncovered for 3 to 5 minutes. Add the eggplants and tamarind, and simmer until half cooked, about 2 minutes. Add the tomato and sugar, and simmer until the tomato is soft, about 2 minutes. Season with the salt and remove from the heat.
3 Transfer to a serving bowl and serve hot, garnished with Crispy Fried Shallots, celery leaves and spring onion.

Serves 4   Preparation time: 20 mins   Cooking time: 15 mins

Classic Grilled Chicken Ayam Panggang

This is one of Indonesia's most traditional dishes and plays an important role in many ceremonies. It is served on special occasions everywhere throughout the archipelago.

1 fresh chicken (2 lbs/1 kg)
2 tablespoons oil
2–3 bird's eye chilies or finger-length chilies
3 stalks lemongrass, thick bottom third only, outer layers discarded, inner part bruised
2$^1/_2$ cups (675 ml) thin coconut milk
2 cups (500 ml) chicken stock or 1 teaspoon chicken stock granules dissolved in 2 cups (500 ml) warm water
2 *salam* leaves (optional)
1 teaspoon salt
1 teaspoon freshly ground black pepper
Sweet Indonesian soy sauce (*kecap manis*), for glazing
1 portion Sambal Kecap (page 33)

Spice Paste
3 candlenuts, roughly chopped
$^1/_2$ in (1 cm) fresh *kencur* root, peeled and sliced (optional)
1 in (2$^1/_2$ cm) fresh galangal, peeled and sliced
1 in (2$^1/_2$ cm) fresh turmeric, peeled and sliced, or 1 teaspoon ground turmeric
4 shallots, peeled
5 cloves garlic, peeled
2 tablespoons shaved palm sugar or dark brown sugar

1 Prepare the Sambal Kecap by following the recipe on page 33.
2 Clean and cut the chicken into serving pieces and press to flatten.
3 Make the Spice Paste by grinding all the ingredients to a smooth paste in a mortar or blender, adding a little oil if necessary to keep the mixture turning.
4 Heat the oil in a wok or large saucepan over medium heat and stir-fry the ground paste, together with the chilies and 2 stalks of the lemongrass until the mixture is fragrant and changes to a golden color, 3 to 5 minutes. Add the coconut milk, chicken stock and remaining lemongrass, and bring to a boil, then reduce the heat to low and simmer uncovered for about 5 minutes. Add the chicken, *salam* leaves (if using), salt and pepper, and continue to simmer for about 30 minutes, turning the chicken frequently in the pan to cook it evenly and allow the spices to penetrate the meat. Turn off the heat and allow the chicken to cool in the sauce to room temperature.
5 Remove the chicken pieces from the sauce and dry in an open, airy place for 30 minutes, then grill the chicken pieces over hot charcoal or under a preheated broiler for 3 to 5 minutes on each side and brush with a little sweet Indonesian soy sauce to glaze the skin. Serve the grilled chicken with steamed rice, vegetables and a bowl of Sambal Kecap on the side.

Serves 4 to 6   Preparation time: 40 mins   Cooking time: 1 hour

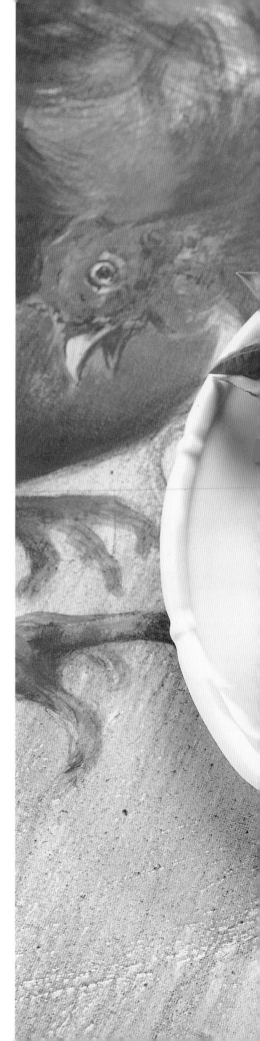

Chicken Simmered in Mild Coconut Gravy   Opor Ayam

A mild dish without chilies but redolent of coriander, lemongrass, *salam* leaves and galangal, Opor Ayam is a universal favorite in Indonesia.

3 cups (750 ml) thin coconut milk
1 fresh chicken (2 lbs/1 kg), cleaned and cut into serving pieces
1 stalk lemongrass, thick bottom third only, outer layers discarded, inner part bruised
2 *salam* leaves
1/2 teaspoon salt
1/2 cup (125 ml) thick coconut milk

Spice Paste
5 candlenuts, roughly chopped
1 in (2 1/2 cm) fresh galangal, peeled and sliced
3 shallots, peeled
3 cloves garlic, peeled
2 tablespoons coriander seeds or 1 tablespoon ground coriander
1 teaspoon ground white pepper
1/2 tablespoon shaved palm sugar or dark brown sugar

1 Make the Spice Paste by grinding all the ingredients to a smooth paste in a mortar or blender, adding a little coconut milk if necessary to keep the mixture turning.
2 Bring the thin coconut milk and Spice Paste to a boil over high heat in a wok or large saucepan. Add the chicken pieces, lemongrass, *salam* leaves and salt, mix well and bring to a boil again. Reduce the heat to low and simmer uncovered for about 30 minutes, until the chicken is cooked and the sauce has reduced by a third. Finally add the thick coconut milk, simmer for 5 more minutes and remove from the heat.
3 Transfer to a serving casserole and garnish with fresh chilies if desired.

Serves 4 to 6   Preparation time: 25 mins   Cooking time: 30 mins

Javanese Fried Chicken   Ayam Goreng Yogya

Seasoned chicken that is simmered in coconut and spices until almost cooked, then flash-fried to give it a crispy coating, make this central Javanese dish a favorite.

Oil, for deep-frying
2 *salam* leaves
1 fresh chicken (2 lbs/1 kg), cleaned and cut into serving pieces
2 cups (500 ml) thin coconut milk
2 limes, cut into wedges, to serve
1 portion Sambal Trasi (page 33)

Spice Paste
1 tablespoon coriander seeds or 2 teaspoons ground coriander
1/2 in (1 cm) fresh galangal, peeled and sliced
1/2 in (1 cm) fresh turmeric, peeled and sliced, or 3/4 teaspoon ground turmeric
3/4 in (2 cm) fresh ginger, peeled and sliced
4–5 shallots, peeled
3 cloves garlic, peeled
1 tablespoon shaved palm sugar or dark brown sugar
1/4 teaspoon salt

1 Prepare the Sambal Trasi by following the recipe on page 33.
2 Make the Spice Paste by grinding all the ingredients to a smooth paste in a mortar or blender, adding a little oil if necessary to keep the mixture turning.
3 Heat 2 tablespoons of the oil in a wok over medium heat and stir-fry the Spice Paste and *salam* leaves until fragrant, 3 to 5 minutes. Add the chicken pieces and stir-fry to coat them well with the spices, then stir in the coconut milk and bring the mixture to a boil. Reduce the heat to low and simmer uncovered until the chicken is almost cooked and the sauce has almost dried up, about 20 minutes. Remove from the heat and set aside to cool.
4 Just before serving, heat the oil in a wok until very hot and deep-fry the chicken until crisp and golden brown on all sides, about 3 minutes. Serve with lime wedges and a small bowl of Sambal Trasi on the side.

Serves 4 to 6   Preparation time: 40 mins   Cooking time: 30 mins

Grilled Chicken with Chili Sauce Ayam Taliwang

Lombok's most famous chicken dish is grilled over a charcoal fire and served with a spicy coconut sauce. This version suggests partially grilling the chicken and finishing it off by deep-frying. Alternatively, the chicken could be deep-fried only, depending on your preference.

1 fresh chicken (about 2 lbs/ 1 kg), cleaned and cut into serving pieces
1 teaspoon salt
1 red finger-length chili, thinly sliced, to garnish
Sprigs of basil leaves, to garnish

Chili Sauce
3–4 red finger-length chilies or 2–3 bird's-eye chilies, deseeded
4 shallots, peeled
1 teaspoon dried shrimp paste (*trasi*), dry-roasted (page 23)
1 teaspoon shaved palm sugar or dark brown sugar
1/4 teaspoon salt
2 tablespoons oil
1 tablespoon freshly squeezed lime or lemon juice

1 Make the Chili Sauce by grinding the chilies, shallots, shrimp paste, sugar and salt in a mortar or blender, adding a little oil if necessary to keep the mixture turning. Heat the oil in a wok or skillet over medium heat and stir-fry the ground paste for 2 to 3 minutes until fragrant. Reduce the heat to low, add the lime or lemon juice and mix well. Remove from the heat and set aside. If prepared in advance, reheat the Chili Sauce just before serving.

2 Season the chicken pieces with the salt and set aside for 5 minutes, then grill the chicken pieces over hot charcoal or under a preheated broiler until half cooked, 2 to 3 minutes. Brush the chicken pieces on both sides with the Chili Sauce and continue to grill for 10 to 15 minutes, basting with the sauce, until cooked. Alternatively, after brushing with the Chili Sauce, deep-fry the chicken pieces in the hot oil until cooked.

3 Spread the remaining Chili Sauce on the cooked chicken. Transfer to a serving platter, garnish with freshly sliced chili and serve with steamed rice.

Serves 4 to 6   Preparation time: 20 mins   Cooking time: 35 mins

Balinese Duck or Chicken Curry Bebek Menyatnyat

Ducks waddling along the banks of rice fields or following the flag held by their owner (or his children) are a common sight in Bali. On festive occasions, duck is a great favorite. Spiced stuffed duck baked in banana leaves (Bebek Betutu) is one popular recipe; this curried duck dish is another. Chicken is also delicious when cooked in this way—which is essentially the Balinese equivalent of a spicy Rendang.

1 fresh duck or roasting chicken
  (about 4 lbs/1³/₄ kg)
2 tablespoons oil
4 cups (1 liter) thick coconut milk
2 stalks lemongrass, thick bottom
  third only, outer layers discarded,
  inner part bruised
2 *salam* leaves (optional)
1 teaspoon salt
1 teaspoon freshly ground black
  pepper

Spice Paste
3 candlenuts, roughly chopped
1 in (2¹/₂ cm) fresh galangal, peeled
  and sliced
1 in (2¹/₂ cm) fresh *kencur root*,
  peeled and sliced
1 in (2¹/₂ cm) fresh turmeric, peeled
  and sliced, or 1 teaspoon ground
  turmeric
2–3 red finger-length chilies, deseeded
8–10 shallots, peeled
6 cloves garlic, peeled
2 cloves
2 teaspoons coriander seeds or 1
  teaspoons ground coriander
¹/₄ teaspoon freshly ground black
  pepper
¹/₄ teaspoon freshly grated nutmeg or
  ground nutmeg
1 teaspoon dried shrimp paste (*trasi*),
  dry-roasted (page 23)

1 Clean and cut the duck or chicken into serving pieces, then dry with paper towels.
2 Make the Spice Paste by grinding all the ingredients in a mortar or blender until fine, adding a little oil if necessary to keep the mixture turning.
3 Heat the oil in a wok over high heat and stir-fry the Spice Paste until fragrant, about 1 minute. Add the duck or chicken pieces and stir-fry for about 3 minutes. Add the coconut milk, lemongrass, *salam* leaves, salt and pepper, mix well and bring to a boil. Reduce the heat to medium low and simmer uncovered, turning frequently, until the duck or chicken pieces are tender and the sauce has thickened, 30 to 35 minutes. Remove from the heat. Garnish with Crispy Fried Shallots and serve with fragrant steamed rice.

Serves 6 to 8   Preparation time: 30 mins   Cooking time: 40 mins

Buginese Chicken Stew   Ayam Masak Bugis

A Buginese favorite from Southern Sulawesi, this dish is prepared by simmering a whole chicken in seasoned stock and coconut milk.

1 fresh chicken (about 2 lbs/1 kg)
4 cups (1 liter) chicken stock or 2 teaspoons chicken stock granules
   dissolved in 4 cups (1 liter) warm water
2 cloves garlic, peeled and sliced
12 shallots, peeled and sliced
1 tablespoon dried shrimp paste (*trasi*), dry-roasted (page 23)
2 tablespoons tamarind juice (page 26)
1 teaspoon ground white pepper
2 *salam* leaves
1 cinnamon stick
4 cloves
$1/4$ teaspoon freshly grated nutmeg or ground nutmeg
1 teaspoon salt
1 teaspoon shaved palm sugar or dark brown sugar
1 tablespoon white vinegar
1 cup (250 ml) thick coconut milk
Crispy Fried Shallots (page 34), to garnish (optional)

1 Prepare the Crispy Fried Shallots (if using) by following the recipe on page 34.
2 Clean and cut the chicken into serving pieces.
3 Bring the chicken stock to a boil over medium heat in a pot. Add all the ingredients, except the chicken and coconut milk, return to a boil and simmer uncovered for 3 to 5 minutes. Add the chicken and coconut milk and bring to a boil again, then simmer uncovered, turning the chicken from time to time until tender and cooked, about 20 minutes.
4 Remove the chicken from the pot and place in a deep platter. Continue to simmer the sauce for 5 to 10 more minutes, until it reduces to half.
5 Pour the sauce over the chicken, garnish with Crispy Fried Shallots and serve with fragrant steamed rice.

Note: For a complete one-pot meal, you can add vegetables like green beans, baby corn, celery, mushrooms, carrots, potatoes, tomatoes and spring onions to the sauce (in Step 4) and simmer until the sauce is thickened.

Serves 4   Preparation time: 25 mins   Cooking time: 40 mins

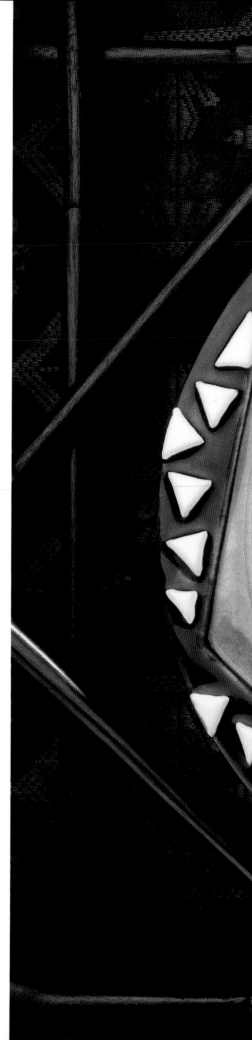

Chicken with Green Tomatoes and Sambal
Ayam Cincane

This recipe comes from Kalimantan, where it is usually made with free-range or *kampung* chickens. The sour tomatoes and lemon juice makes a delicious counterpoint to the sweet spiciness of the special sambal that is served with this dish.

1 fresh chicken (2 lbs/1 kg)
1 teaspoon salt
1 tablespoon freshly squeezed lime or lemon juice
2 cups (500 ml) water
3–4 red finger-length chilies, deseeded and sliced
8–10 shallots, peeled and sliced
4 unripe tomatoes, sliced
1 sprig Asian basil
3 kaffir lime leaves
2 spring onions, sliced
1/2 in (1 cm) fresh ginger, peeled and sliced

Fragrant Chili Sambal
1/4 teaspoon freshly grated nutmeg or ground nutmeg
3–4 red finger-length chilies, deseeded
5–6 shallots, peeled
3 cloves garlic, peeled
1 teaspoon salt
2 tablespoons shaved palm sugar or dark brown sugar
1 teaspoon dried shrimp paste (*trasi*), dry-roasted (page 23)
1 tablespoon oil
1 *salam* leaf
1 stalk lemongrass, thick bottom third only, outer layers discarded, inner part bruised
1/2 in (1 cm) fresh galangal, peeled and sliced
2 tablespoons tamarind juice (page 25)

1 Clean and cut the chicken into serving pieces. Season the chicken pieces with the salt and lime or lemon juice, then set aside to marinate for at least 20 minutes.
2 Make the Fragrant Chili Sambal by grinding the first 7 ingredients to a smooth paste in a mortar or blender, adding a little oil if necessary to keep the mixture turning. Heat the oil in a wok or skillet over medium heat and stir-fry the ground paste with the *salam* leaf, lemongrass and galangal until fragrant, 3 to 5 minutes. Add the tamarind juice and bring the mixture to a boil, then reduce the heat to low and simmer for about 1 minute. Remove from the heat and set aside to cool. Discard the *salam* leaf, lemongrass and galangal.
3 Bring the water to a boil in a wok or large saucepan. Add the marinated chicken and simmer uncovered over medium heat until the chicken is just tender, 5 to 10 minutes. Add all the other ingredients, mix well and cook for 15 more minutes before removing from the heat. Serve immediately with a serving bowl of Fragrant Chili Sambal on the side or serve mixed with the Fragrant Chili Sambal.

Serves 4 to 6   Preparation time: 45 mins   Cooking time: 40 mins

Eggs in Fragrant Lemongrass Sauce   Telur Petis

8 eggs
1 tablespoon oil
1 teaspoon palm sugar or dark brown
   sugar
2 cups (500 ml) thick coconut milk
2 bird's-eye chilies, bruised
2 stalks lemongrass, thick bottom
   third only, outer layers discarded,
   inner part bruised
2 *salam* leaves
1/2 teaspoon salt
Crispy Fried Shallots (page 34),
   to garnish (optional)

Spice Paste
1/2 in (1 cm) fresh galangal, peeled
   and sliced
1/2 in (1 cm) fresh turmeric, peeled
   and sliced, or 1/2 teaspoon ground
   turmeric
3–4 red finger-length chilies,
   deseeded
4–5 shallots, peeled
3 cloves garlic, peeled
1 teaspoon dried shrimp paste (*trasi*),
   dry-roasted (page 23)

1 Prepare the Crispy Fried Shallots (if using) by following the recipe on page 34.
2 Boil the eggs for 7 to 8 minutes until hard, then drain and plunge into a basin of cold water to cool. Peel the eggs and set aside.
3 Prepare the Spice Paste by grinding all the ingredients in a mortar or blender until fine and adding a little coconut milk if necessary to keep the mixture turning. Set aside.
4 Heat the oil in a wok over medium heat and stir-fry the Spice Paste until fragrant, 3 to 5 minutes. Add the sugar and stir-fry until completely dissolved, then add the coconut milk, chilies, lemongrass and *salam* leaves and bring to a boil, stirring gently. Reduce the heat to low, add the eggs and simmer uncovered until the sauce thickens, 8 to 10 minutes. Season with the salt and remove from the heat. Garnish with Crispy Fried Shallots and serve hot with steamed rice.

Serves 4 to 6   Preparation time: 30 mins   Cooking time: 30 mins

Spicy Padang-style Eggs   Gulai Telur

8 eggs
2 cups (500 ml) thick coconut milk
1/2 turmeric leaf, shredded (optional)
1 tablespoon tamarind juice (page 26)
1/2 teaspoon salt
Crispy Fried Shallots (page 34),
   to garnish (optional)

Spice Paste
1 in (2 1/2 cm) fresh galangal, peeled
   and sliced
1/2 in (1 cm) fresh turmeric, peeled
   and sliced, or 1/2 teaspoon ground
   turmeric
1 in (2 1/2 cm) fresh ginger, peeled
   and sliced
2–4 bird's-eye chilies, deseeded
5 shallots, peeled
3 cloves garlic, peeled

1 Prepare the Crispy Fried Shallots (if using) by following the recipe on page 34.
2 Boil the eggs for 7 to 8 minutes until hard, then drain and plunge into a basin of cold water to cool. Peel the eggs and set aside.
3 Prepare the Spice Paste by grinding all the ingredients coarsely in a mortar or blender and adding a little coconut milk if necessary to keep the mixture turning. Set aside.
4 Bring the coconut milk slowly to a boil in a wok or saucepan. Add the Spice Paste and turmeric leaf (if using), mix well and simmer for 2 minutes. Reduce the heat to low, add the eggs and continue to simmer uncovered until the sauce thickens, 8 to 10 minutes. Season with the tamarind juice and salt, simmer for 1 more minute and remove from the heat. Serve hot garnished with Crispy Fried Shallots.

Serves 4 to 6   Preparation time: 25 mins   Cooking time: 25 mins

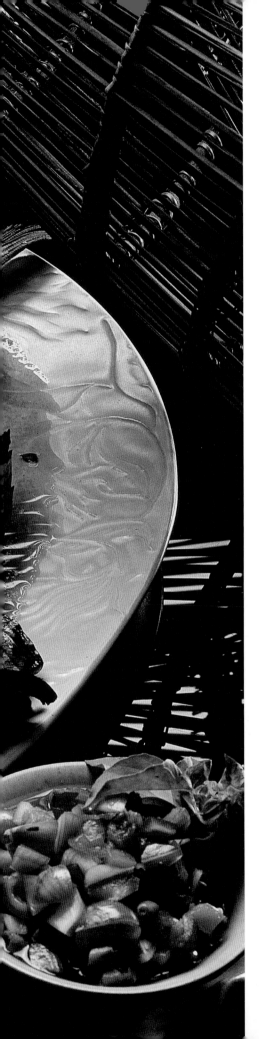

Grilled Fish with Basil and Tomato Sambal
Ikan Bakar Colo Colo

Fish, grilled plain or wrapped in banana leaves, is very popular on the eastern Indonesian islands of Sulawesi and Maluku. This recipe from Maluku is very simple—flavored with a typical Colo Colo Sambal.

2 1 whole fresh fish (about 2 lbs/1 kg), or 1$^1/_2$ lbs (700 g) fish steaks
$^1/_2$ teaspoon salt
1 tablespoon freshly squeezed lime or lemon juice
2 tablespoons oil
1 large banana leaf or aluminum foil, for wrapping

Colo Colo Sambal
3–4 red finger-length chilies or bird's-eye chilies, deseeded and sliced
4 shallots, peeled and sliced
2 ripe tomatoes, diced
4 sprigs Asian basil, minced
4 tablespoons sweet Indonesian soy sauce (*kecap manis*)
2 tablespoons freshly squeezed lime or lemon juice

1 If using whole fish, scale, gut and clean the fish, then make several shallow diagonal slits on each side. Season the fish with the salt and lime or lemon juice, then brush it with the oil. Set aside for 15 minutes.
2 Make the Colo Colo Sambal by combining all the ingredients in a bowl and mixing well.
3 Scald the banana leaf in a basin by pouring boiling water over it, then wipe it dry. Wrap the seasoned fish in the banana leaf or aluminum foil. Cook the parcel directly over hot charcoal or under a preheated broiler until the banana leaf is evenly browned and the fish is done, 10 to 15 minutes on each side.
4 Unwrap the fish parcel and spoon the sambal over it. Serve immediately. Alternatively serve the Colo Colo Sambal in a small bowl on the side.

Serves 4   Preparation time: 20 mins   Cooking time: 30 mins

Lemongrass Tamarind Fish   Arsin Ikan Mas

With plentiful lakes and rivers, Sumatra is the source of many delicious freshwater fish recipes, including this one.

2 lbs (1 kg) freshwater fish such as carp or trout, either whole fish or fillets
1 teaspoon salt
1 teaspoon ground white pepper
2 cups (500 ml) water
2 stalks lemongrass, thick bottom third only, outer layers discarded,
 inner part bruised
2 tablespoons tamarind juice (page 26)
1 spring onion, sliced, to garnish
2 limes or $^1/_2$ lemon, cut into wedges, to serve

Spice Paste
6 candlenuts, roughly chopped
1 in (2$^1/_2$ cm) fresh galangal, peeled and sliced
1 in (2$^1/_2$ cm) fresh turmeric, peeled and sliced,
 or 1 teaspoon ground turmeric
1 in (2$^1/_2$ cm) fresh ginger, peeled and sliced
2–3 red finger-length chilies, deseeded
4–5 shallots, peeled
4 cloves garlic, peeled
$^1/_2$ teaspoon salt

1 If using whole fish, scale, gut and clean the fish, then make several shallow diagonal slits on each side. Season the fish with the salt and pepper, and set aside for 15 minutes.
2 Make the Spice Paste by grinding all the ingredients to a smooth paste in a mortar or blender, adding a little water if necessary to keep the mixture turning.
3 Bring the Spice Paste, water, lemongrass and tamarind juice to a boil in a wok or skillet. Reduce the heat to medium and simmer uncovered for about 10 minutes, adding more water if the sauce evaporates too quickly. Add the fish, cover and simmer until cooked, 6 to 10 minutes, turning the fish over from time to time to cook it evenly on both sides. Remove from the heat.
4 Transfer the fish to a serving platter and pour the sauce over it. Garnish with sliced spring onion and serve hot with lime or lemon wedges.

Serves 4   Preparation time: 25 mins   Cooking time: 25 mins

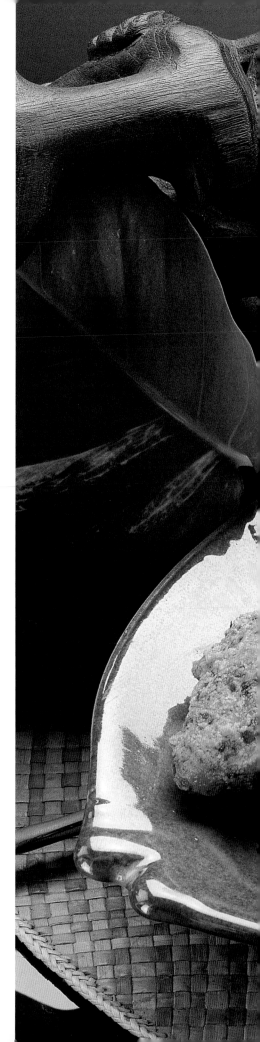

Shrimp in Hot Coconut Sauce Sambal Petai Udang

1 lb (500 g) fresh medium shrimp
4–5 pods stinkbeans (*petai*) (optional)
2 tablespoons oil
2 cups (500 ml) thin coconut milk
2 medium potatoes, peeled, halved
  and sliced
1 carrot, peeled and sliced
2 red finger-length chilies, deseeded
  and sliced (optional)
2 tablespoons tamarind juice (page 26)
1 tablespoon sugar (optional)
1 teaspoon salt
Crispy Fried Shallots (page 34), to
  garnish

Spice Paste
3–4 red finger-length chilies, deseeded
5 shallots, peeled
3 cloves garlic, peeled
$1/_2$ teaspoon dried shrimp paste
  (*trasi*), dry-roasted (page 23)

1 Prepare the Crispy Fried Shallots by following the recipe on page 34.
2 Peel and devein the shrimp. Open the stinkbean pods and reserve the beans, about 35 of them. Discard the pods.
3 To make the Spice Paste, grind all the ingredients to a smooth paste in a mortar or blender, adding a little oil if necessary to keep the mixture turning.
4 Heat the oil in a wok over medium heat and stir-fry the Spice Paste until fragrant, 3 to 5 minutes. Add the stinkbeans (if using) and coconut milk and bring to a boil, stirring gently. Add the sliced potato, carrot, chili (if using) and tamarind juice, and mix well. Bring the ingredients to a boil again and simmer uncovered until the vegetables are cooked and the sauce has thickened, 3 to 5 minutes. Add the shrimp and simmer for 2 to 3 minutes until the shrimp turn pink. Season with the sugar (if using) and salt, and remove from the heat.
5 Transfer to a serving platter, garnish with Crispy Fried Shallots and serve hot with steamed rice.

Note: *Petai* belong to the legume family. The long, green pods enclose 6 to 8 pungent beans that are called stinkbeans in English because they have a very pungent odor. They are sold without the pods in bottles or in vacuum-sealed bags in Asian supermarkets.

Serves 4 to 6   Preparation time: 25 mins   Cooking time: 20 mins

Lobsters in Yellow Sauce   Udang Pantung Kuning

4 small lobsters (about 1 lb/500 g each)
6 cups (1$^1/_2$ liters) water
2 stalks lemongrass, thick bottom
   third only, outer layers discarded,
   inner part bruised
2 kaffir lime leaves
$^1/_4$ teaspoon white vinegar
1$^1/_2$ cups (375 ml) coconut cream
1 teaspoon salt
Crispy Fried Shallots (page 34)

Spice Paste
3 candlenuts, roughly chopped
2–3 red finger-length chilies
4–5 shallots, peeled
3 cloves garlic, peeled
2 in (5 cm) fresh turmeric, peeled and
   sliced, or 2 teaspoons ground turmeric
2 in (5 cm) ginger, peeled and sliced
1$^1/_2$ teaspoons coriander seeds
$^1/_2$ teaspoon dried shrimp paste
   (*trasi*), dry-roasted (page 23)
2 tablespoons oil
1 *salam* leaf or bay leaf
2 tablespoons tamarind juice (page 26)

1 Prepare the Crispy Fried Shallots by following the recipe on page 34.
2 Scrub and clean the lobsters. Bring the water to a boil over medium heat in a pot, add the lobsters and boil for 10 to 15 minutes. Remove the lobsters from the heat and immediately plunge them into a basin of iced water for 1 minute to cool. Strain and reserve the stock. Drain the lobsters and remove the meat from the shells. Discard the shells.
3 Prepare the Spice Paste by grinding all the ingredients (except the oil, *salam* leaf and tamarind juice) to a smooth paste in a mortar or blender, adding a little oil if necessary to keep the mixture turning. Heat the oil over medium heat in a wok or skillet and stir-fry the Spice Paste until fragrant, 3 to 5 minutes. Add the *salam* leaf and tamarind juice and simmer for about 2 minutes, then remove from the heat. Set aside.
4 In a pot, bring the lobster stock, Spice Paste, lemongrass, lime leaves and vinegar to a boil over medium heat, then simmer uncovered for 3 to 5 minutes. Add the coconut cream, mix well and bring to a boil again, then simmer for about 5 minutes. Finally add the lobster meat, season with the salt and simmer for 1 minute. Remove from the heat.
5 Transfer to a serving bowl, garnish with Crispy Fried Shallots and serve hot with steamed rice.

Serves 4   Preparation time: 30 mins   Cooking time: 35 mins

Fried Fish with Tomato Sambal   Ikan Bumbu Acar

Small fresh fish like sardines, are used in this typical seafood dish from fishing village near Pekalongan, on the northern coast of Central Java.

1¹/₂ lbs (700 g) small fresh fish, gut
  and cleaned, then left whole, or fish
  steaks
1 teaspoon salt
5 tablespoons oil
2 red finger-length chilies, deseeded
  and sliced (optional)
3 shallots, peeled and sliced
2 cloves garlic, peeled and sliced
2 ripe tomatoes, cut into wedges
1 *salam* leaf
2 tablespoons tamarind juice (page
  26)
2 teaspoons sugar
Pinch of salt
¹/₂ teaspoon ground white pepper
3 tablespoons water
Sprigs of Lemon Basil, to garnish

Spice Paste
2 candlenuts, roughly chopped
3–4 red finger-length chilies,
  deseeded
6 shallots, peeled
2 cloves garlic, peeled
¹/₂ in (1 cm) fresh galangal, peeled
  and sliced
1 in (2¹/₂ cm) fresh ginger, peeled
  and sliced
1 in (2¹/₂ cm) fresh turmeric, peeled
  and sliced, or 1 teaspoon ground
  turmeric
¹/₂ teaspoon ground coriander

1 Season the fish with the salt and set aside for 15 minutes.
2 Prepare the Spice Paste by grinding all the ingredients to a smooth paste in a mortar or blender, adding a little oil if necessary to keep the mixture turning. Set aside.
3 Heat 3 tablespoons of the oil in a wok over medium heat until hot. Pan-fry the seasoned fish until golden brown and crispy, 5 to 7 minutes. Remove from the pan and drain on paper towels.
4 Heat the remaining oil over medium heat in a wok and stir-fry the Spice Paste until fragrant, 3 to 5 minutes. Add the sliced chili (if using), shallot and garlic, tomato wedges, *salam* leaf and tamarind juice, and stir-fry for 1 minute, then season with the sugar, salt and pepper. Finally add the fried fish and water, mix well and simmer for 1 minute before removing from the heat.
5 Transfer to a serving platter, garnish with basil leaves and serve hot.

Serves 4 to 6   Preparation time: 30 mins   Cooking time: 15 mins

Fish Stew with Lemongrass and Turmeric

This dish is typically cooked with fish heads in Indonesia, as shown in the photo above, but is equally delicious with whole fish or fillets.

1¹/₂ lbs (700 g) whole snapper, tuna or sea bream, or fish fillets
1 tablespoon oil
4 cups (1 liter) water
1 teaspoon salt
3 stalks lemongrass, thick bottom third only, outer layers discarded, inner part bruised
5 kaffir lime leaves
1–2 red finger-length chilies, sliced
2 spring onions, cut into lengths
Crispy Fried Shallots (page 34)

Spice Paste
1¹/₂ in (4 cm) fresh turmeric, peeled and sliced, or 1¹/₂ teaspoons ground turmeric
2 in (5 cm) ginger, peeled and sliced
2–3 red finger-length chilies, deseeded
4–6 shallots, peeled
3 cloves garlic, peeled

1 If using whole fish, scale, gut and clean the fish, then make several shallow diagonal slits on each side.
2 Make the Spice Paste by grinding all the ingredients to a smooth paste in a mortar or blender, adding a little water if necessary to keep the mixture turning.
3 Heat the oil in a wok over high heat and stir-fry the Spice Paste for 1 to 2 minutes until fragrant. Add the water, salt, lemongrass and kaffir lime leaves, and bring to a boil. Add the fish, reduce the heat to medium and return to a boil, then simmer uncovered until the fish is cooked, 7 to 10 minutes. Adjust the taste with more salt or water as desired and remove from the heat.
4 Transfer to a serving platter and serve hot with steamed rice, garnished with sliced chili, spring onions and Crispy Fried Shallots (if using).

Serves 4   Preparation time: 20 mins   Cooking time: 15 mins

Beef Soup with Chilies and Tamarind   Daging Belacan

This soup from Timor in eastern Indonesia has a wonderful sweet-sour edge to it.

8 cups (2 liters) water
2 lbs (1 kg) top round or stewing beef
3 tablespoons oil
4–5 shallots, peeled
2 cloves garlic, peeled
1 teaspoon dried shrimp paste (*trasi*),
  dry-roasted (page 23)
2 tablespoons shaved palm sugar or
  dark brown sugar
1 tablespoon sweet Indonesian soy
  sauce (*kecap manis*)
2 tablespoons tamarind juice (page 26)
1 teaspoon salt
1–2 red finger-length chilies,
  deseeded and sliced into strips
2 spring onions, cut into short lengths

1 Bring the water to a boil in a large pot. Add the beef, reduce the heat to low and simmer until the meat is half cooked, about 15 minutes. Turn off the heat. Remove the beef from the stock and drain. Strain and reserve the stock.
2 When cool enough to handle, cut the beef into cubes. Heat 2 tablespoons of the oil over medium heat in a skillet and pan-fry the beef until cooked, 2 to 3 minutes. Remove from the heat and set aside.
3 Grind the shallots, garlic, dried shrimp paste and sugar to a smooth paste in a mortar or blender, adding a little water if necessary to keep the mixture turning. Set aside.
4 Heat the remaining oil in a wok over medium heat and stir-fry the ground paste until fragrant, 3 to 5 minutes. Add the beef cubes and sweet Indonesian soy sauce, and stir-fry for 2 minutes, then pour in the reserved beef stock and tamarind juice, and season with the salt. Bring the soup to a boil, then simmer uncovered until the beef is tender, 10 to 15 minutes. Adjust the taste with more salt or tamarind juice as desired, stir in the sliced chilies and spring onions, and remove from the heat. Serve hot.

Serves 4 to 6   Preparation time: 20 mins   Cooking time: 45 mins

Beef Rendang   Spicy Beef in Coconut

This is one of the most popular Indonesian dishes, which originated in Padang, West Sumatra, and features chunks of beef stewed in coconut and spices.

2 lbs (1 kg) top round or stewing beef
2 tablespoons oil
2 cups (500 ml) coconut cream or 3 cups (750 ml) thick coconut milk
3 *salam* leaves
3 kaffir lime leaves
3 fresh turmeric leaves (optional)
1 cinnamon stick
2 tablespoons shaved palm sugar or dark brown sugar
2 teaspoons salt
Crispy Fried Shallots (page 34), to garnish

Spice Paste
1 teaspoon black peppercorns
3 in (8 cm) fresh galangal, peeled and sliced
2 stalks lemongrass, thick bottom third only, outer layers discarded,
  inner part sliced
2 in (5 cm) fresh ginger, peeled and sliced
3–4 red finger-length chilies, deseeded
8–10 shallots, peeled
8–10 cloves garlic, peeled

1 Prepare the Crispy Fried Shallots by following the recipe on page 34.
2 Cut the beef into bite-sized chunks and set aside.
3 Make the Spice Paste by grinding all the ingredients very coarsely in a mortar or blender, adding a little coconut cream if necessary to keep the mixture turning.
4 Heat the oil in a wok over high heat and stir-fry the Spice Paste until fragrant, 1 to 2 minutes. Add the beef chunks and all the other ingredients, except the Crispy Fried Shallots, and bring to a boil, stirring constantly. Reduce the heat to medium and simmer uncovered for about 1 hour, then reduce the heat to low and continue simmering for 1 more hour, stirring from time to time until the meat is very tender and most of the liquid has evaporated. By this time, the oil will have separated from the milk. Continue to stir-fry the beef in this oil for about 25 minutes until it turns a dark brown color, then remove from the heat.
5 Transfer the beef to a serving platter, garnish with Crispy Fried Shallots and serve with steamed rice. This dish actually tastes better if left to sit for several hours, or even overnight in the refrigerator, then stir-fry it again for several minutes to reheat, and serve.

Serves 4 to 6   Preparation time: 30 mins   Cooking time: 2 hours 30 mins

Lamb Satay   Sate Madura

Normally made with goat meat, this is probably the most popular type of satay in Indonesia, originating from the island of Madura just to the northeast of Java.

1½ lbs (750 g) boneless lamb
24 bamboo skewers, soaked in water for 4 hours before using
Lime wedges, to serve
1 portion Sambal Kecap (page 33)
1 portion Sambal Kacang (page 34)

Marinade
½ cup (125 ml) sweet Indonesian soy sauce (kecap manis)
½ teaspoon coriander seeds, crushed, or ½ teaspoon ground coriander
¼ teaspoon ground white pepper
1 tablespoon freshly squeezed lime or lemon juice

1 Cut the lamb into bite-sized cubes. Combine the Marinade ingredients in a bowl and mix well. Pour two-third of the Marinade to the meat cubes, mix until well coated and allow to marinate for at least 2 hours. Reserve the remaining Marinade.
2 Prepare the Sambal Kecap and Sambal Kacang by following the recipes on pages 33 and 34. Set aside.
3 Thread the marinated meat cubes onto the bamboo skewers and grill over hot charcoal or under a preheated broiler for 5 to 7 minutes, turning and basting frequently with the reserved Marinade, until the meat is well cooked and browned on all sides. Arrange the satays on a serving platter and serve with the lime wedges and bowls of Sambal Kecap and Sambal Kacang on the side.

Makes 24 satays or serves 4 to 6   Preparation time: 30 mins + 2 hours to marinate
Cooking time: 15 mins

Lombok-style Marinated Beef Satay   Sate Ampet Sasak

In Lombok, as in neighboring Bali, satay meat is usually highly seasoned and marinated before grilling.

2 lbs (1 kg) beef sirloin
24 bamboo skewers, soaked in water for 4 hours before using
Lime or lemon wedges, to serve
1 portion Sambal Kecap (page 34)

Marinade
4 candlenuts, roughly chopped
1 in (2½ cm) fresh ginger, peeled and sliced
2 red finger-length chilies, deseeded
2–3 bird's-eye chilies, deseeded
5 cloves garlic, peeled
½ teaspoon dried shrimp paste (trasi), dry-roasted (page 23)
1 teaspoon salt
2 tablespoons oil
1 cups (250 ml) thick coconut milk

1 Cut the beef into bite-sized cubes and set aside.
2 Prepare the Marinade by grinding all the ingredients (except the oil and coconut milk) to a smooth paste in a mortar or blender and adding a little oil if necessary to keep the mixture turning. Heat the oil in a wok over medium heat and stir-fry the ground paste until fragrant, 3 to 5 minutes. Reduce the heat to low, add the coconut milk and simmer until the Marinade has thickened, about 10 minutes. Remove from the heat and set aside to cool. Pour the Marinade over the beef cubes in a large bowl, mix until well coated and allow to marinate for at least 2 hours.
3 Prepare the Sambal Kecap by following the recipe on page 34.
4 Thread the marinated beef cubes onto the bamboo skewers and grill over hot charcoal or under a preheated broiler for 5 to 7 minutes, turning and basting frequently with the Marinade, until the meat is well cooked and browned on all sides. Arrange the satays on a serving platter and serve with the lime or lemon wedges and a bowl of Sambal Kecap on the side.

Makes 24 satays or serves 4 to 6   Preparation time: 25 mins + 2 hours to marinate
Cooking time: 30 mins

Seasoned Fried Beef Slices Lapis Manado

As the Indonesian name of this dish implies, it comes from Manado, in Northern Sulawesi.

1$^{1}/_{2}$ lbs (700 g) sirloin beef
3 cloves
$^{1}/_{4}$ teaspoon freshly grated nutmeg or ground nutmeg
1 teaspoon salt
2 cups (500 ml) water
Oil, for deep-frying

Spice Paste
6–8 red finger-length chilies, deseeded
1 in (2$^{1}/_{2}$ cm) fresh *kencur* root, peeled and sliced
1 in (2$^{1}/_{2}$ cm) fresh turmeric, peeled and sliced,
  or 1 teaspoon ground turmeric
1 in (2$^{1}/_{2}$ cm) fresh ginger, peeled and sliced
2 teaspoons coriander seeds, or 1 teaspoon ground coriander
1 teaspoon ground white pepper

1 Prepare the Spice Paste by grinding all the ingredients to a smooth paste in a mortar or blender, adding a little water if necessary to keep the mixture turning.
2 Heat 1 tablespoon of the oil in a wok over medium heat and stir-fry the Spice Paste until fragrant, 3 to 5 minutes. Add the beef, cloves, nutmeg, salt and water and bring to a boil, then simmer uncovered for 3 to 5 minutes, until the beef is half cooked. Remove the beef from the pan and continue to simmer the stock for 5 more minutes until it thickens, then turn off the heat. Slice the beef into thin strips.
3 Heat the oil in a wok over high heat until hot. Deep-fry the beef strips for 2 to 3 minutes until browned and cooked. Remove from the hot oil and drain on paper towels. Arrange the beef on a serving platter and pour the gravy over it. Serve immediately.

Serves 4 to 6   Preparation time: 15 mins   Cooking time: 15 mins

Beef with Coconut Hagape Daging

A coconut-rich beef dish from Ambon, in the Spice Islands of Maluku, which unlike similar dishes from Java and Sumatra has no chili, sugar and soy sauce. Nevertheless, the combination of coconut with galangal, lemongrass, turmeric and ginger gives this dish a wonderfully complete aroma and flavor.

2 lbs (1 kg) top round or stewing beef
1 cup (100 g) freshly grated coconut
   or 1 cup (80 g) unsweetened desiccated coconut
2 tablespoons oil
2¹/₂ cups (675 ml) thick coconut milk
1 stalk lemongrass, thick bottom
   third only, outer layers discarded,
   inner part bruised

Spice Paste
6 candlenuts, roughly chopped
2 in (5 cm) fresh galangal, peeled
   and sliced
3 in (8 cm) fresh turmeric, peeled
   and sliced, or 1 tablespoon ground
   turmeric
3 in (8 cm) fresh ginger, peeled and
   sliced
¹/₂ teaspoon coriander seeds
¹/₂ teaspoon ground white pepper
1 teaspoon salt

1 Slice the beef into bite-sized chunks.
2 Dry-fry the grated coconut or desiccated coconut in a skillet over low heat until golden brown, stirring frequently, about 10 minutes for fresh grated coconut or 5 to 8 minutes for desiccated coconut. Remove from the heat and allow to cool. While still warm, grind the coconut in a mortar or blender until fine. Set aside.
3 Prepare the Spice Paste by grinding all the ingredients to a smooth paste in a mortar or blender, adding a little oil if necessary to keep the mixture turning. Set aside.
4 Heat the oil in a wok over medium heat and stir-fry the Spice Paste until fragrant, 3 to 5 minutes. Add the beef, ground coconut, coconut milk and lemongrass, mix well and bring to a boil, then simmer uncovered for about 10 minutes, stirring constantly to prevent the coconut milk from separating. Reduce the heat to low and continue to simmer uncovered, stirring from time to time, until the beef is tender and the sauce has almost dried up, about 30 minutes. Add a little water if the sauce dries up before the meat is cooked. Remove from the heat.
5 Transfer to a serving platter and serve hot with steamed rice.

Serves 6 to 8   Preparation time: 20 mins   Cooking time: 1 hour

Corn Rice Nasi Jagung

Corn is often used to add bulk to rice in areas where rice is costly or difficult to obtain. Dried corn should be soaked for 24 hours before using, although this is unnecessary if using fresh or canned sweet corn.

1¹/₂ cups (300 g) uncooked rice,
   washed thoroughly and drained
1¹/₂ cups (360 g) sweet corn kernels,
   cut from fresh cobs,
   or one 15-oz (425-g) can sweet
   corn kernels, drained
3¹/₂ cups (875 ml) water

1 Bring all the ingredients to a boil in a pot. If using canned sweet corn, do not add at this stage. Reduce the heat to medium and simmer until the water has almost dried up, 5 to 7 minutes. If using canned sweet corn, add the corn to the rice now.
2 Reduce the heat to low and continue cooking the rice for 10 more minutes, stirring from time to time to prevent burning, until the rice is dry and fluffy. Remove from the heat, stir well and serve hot.

Serves 4 to 6   Preparation time: 5 mins   Cooking time: 20 mins

Makassarese Sparerib Soup   Konro Makasar

The Makassarese of Southern Sulawesi are renowned for their hearty beef soups with lemongrass and coconut.

2 lbs (1 kg) meaty beef spareribs, ribs separated and cut into lengths
3 cups (300 g) freshly grated coconut,
  or 2 cups (150 g) unsweetened desiccated coconut
16 cups (4 liters) water
3 stalks lemongrass, thick bottom third only, outer layers discarded,
  inner part bruised
1 in (2$^1/_2$ cm) fresh galangal, peeled and sliced
3 kaffir lime leaves
1 teaspoon ground white pepper
1 teaspoon salt
Crispy Fried Shallots (page 34), to garnish

Spice Paste
3 candlenuts, roughly chopped
3–4 shallots, peeled
2 cloves garlic, peeled

1 Prepare the Crispy Fried Shallots by following the recipe on page 34.
2 Separate the beef ribs and cut into lengths. Set aside.
3 Dry-fry the grated coconut in a skillet over low heat, stirring constantly until it turns golden brown, about 10 minutes for fresh coconut and 5 to 7 minutes for desiccated coconut. Remove from the heat and allow to cool. While still warm, grind the coconut in a mortar or blender until fine. Set aside.
4 Prepare the Spice Paste by grinding all the ingredients to a smooth paste in a mortar or blender, adding a little water if necessary to keep the mixture turning. Set aside.
5 Bring the beef and water to a boil in a large pot and simmer uncovered over medium heat until the beef is tender, 30 to 40 minutes. Add the ground coconut, Spice Paste and all the remaining ingredients (except the Crispy Fried Shallots), mix well and continue to simmer for 15 more minutes, until the beef is very tender, but not falling off the bones. Remove from the heat and serve garnished with the Crispy Fried Shallots.

Serves 4 to 6   Preparation time: 20 mins   Cooking time: 1 hour 5 mins

Pork Stewed with Tomatoes Babi Masak Tomat

A simple recipe from Kalimantan, where pork (particularly wild boar from the jungle) is popular among the Dyaks.

1 1/2 lbs (700 g) pork
4 ripe tomatoes, cut into wedges
4–6 garlic chives (*kucai*) or spring
  onions, cut into lengths
1 stalk lemongrass, thick bottom third
  only, outer layers discarded, inner
  part bruised
1 cup (250 ml) water

Spice Paste
1 in (2 1/2 cm) fresh ginger, peeled
  and sliced
2–3 red finger-length chilies, deseeded
4 shallots, peeled

1 Cut the pork into bite-sized chunks.
2 Grind the Spice Paste ingredients to a smooth paste in a mortar or blender, adding a little water if necessary to keep the mixture turning.
3 Bring the Spice Paste and all the other ingredients to a boil in a wok or saucepan, then simmer over medium heat until the pork is tender, 3 to 5 minutes, adding a little sugar if the tomatoes are quite sour and a little water if the sauce dries up before the meat is cooked. Remove from the heat and serve immediately with steamed rice.

Serves 4 to 6   Preparation time: 15 mins   Cooking time: 5 mins

Menadonese Ginger Pork Tinaransay

In Northern Sulawesi, where many of the population are Christians and Chinese, the Muslim strictures on eating pork do not apply.

1 1/2 lbs (700 g) boneless pork
  shoulder or leg
2 1/2 in (6 cm) fresh ginger, peeled
  and sliced
2–3 red finger-length chilies,
  deseeded
3 shallots, peeled
2 tablespoons oil
5 kaffir lime leaves
2 turmeric leaves (optional)
3 stalks lemongrass, thick bottom
  third only, outer layers discarded,
  inner part bruised and sliced
1/2 teaspoon salt

1 Cut the pork into bite-sized chunks. Set aside.
2 Grind the ginger, chilies and shallots coarsely in a mortar or blender, adding a little water if necessary to keep the mixture turning. Set aside.
3 Heat the oil in wok over medium heat and stir-fry the ground mixture until fragrant, 3 to 5 minutes. Add the pork and all the other ingredients and stir-fry for about 2 minutes, then reduce the heat to low, cover the wok and simmer the pork in its own juices until tender, 3 to 5 minutes. Add a little warm water if the gravy dries up before the meat is cooked. Remove from the heat and serve with steamed rice.

Serves 4 to 6   Preparation time: 15 mins   Cooking time: 15 mins

Balinese Black Rice Pudding   Bubur Injin

It's hard to find a foreign visitor to Bali who does not fall in love with the wonderful nutty flavor and melt-in-your-mouth smooth texture of Black Rice Pudding, served with swirls of delicious coconut cream on top.

1 cup (200 g) uncooked black gluti-nous rice (see note)
³/₄ cup (150 g) uncooked white gluti-nous rice
6 cups (1¹/₂ liters) water
2 pandanus leaves, tied into a knot, or 1 drop vanilla extract
¹/₄ cup (50 g) shaved palm sugar or dark brown sugar
Pinch of salt
¹/₂ cup (125 ml) coconut cream

1 Rinse both types of glutinous rice in several changes of water until water runs clear, and soak overnight.
2 In a saucepan, bring the glutinous rice, water and pandanus leaves or extract to a boil over medium heat and simmer uncovered for about 40 minutes, stirring occasionally until the rice is soft and cooked, with porridge-like consistency. Discard the pandanus leaves, if using. Add the palm sugar and stir until the sugar is dissolved. Reduce the heat to low and simmer for about 5 minutes before removing from the heat.
3 Combine the coconut cream and salt in a bowl and mix well.
4 To serve, spoon the pudding into individual serving bowls and top with the salted coconut cream.

Note: **Black glutinous rice** is a variety of glutinous rice found mainly in Indonesia. Normal glutinous rice may be substituted, although the texture is not quite the same.

Serves 6 to 8   Preparation time: 10 mins + overnight soaking
Cooking time: 50 mins

Fried Bananas   Pisang Goreng

There are many ways of cooking bananas in Indonesia. Here are two examples, but you can also add coconut cream to the batter or coat the cooked bananas with grated coconut (as shown on left).

1 cup (125 g) rice flour or plain flour, sifted
$^1/_3$ cup (80 ml) water
$^1/_3$ cup (80 ml) coconut cream
$^1/_4$ teaspoon salt
Oil, for deep-frying
8 small finger bananas, peeled and halved, or 4 regular bananas, peeled, halved and sliced lengthwise

1 Place the flour in a mixing bowl. Make a well in the middle and add the water, coconut cream and salt. Using a wooden spoon or balloon whisk, gradually incorporate the flour into the liquid and whisk to make a smooth thick batter free of lumps, adding more flour or water as needed.
2 Heat the oil in a wok or large saucepan until moderately hot. Dip the banana pieces in the batter to coat thoroughly. Gently lower the coated pieces into the oil, a few at a time, and deep-fry over medium low heat for 5 to 10 minutes, turning occasionally, until golden brown and crispy. Remove from the heat and drain on paper towels. Transfer to a serving platter and serve with vanilla ice cream if desired.
3 Alternatively, prepare the batter as indicated and coat the banana pieces generously. Bring 6 cups (1$^1/_2$ liters) of water, $^1/_4$ teaspoon salt and 1 pandanus leaf to a boil. Add the coated banana pieces, reduce the heat and boil over very low heat for about 5 minutes. Remove the banana pieces from the water and drain, then coat with freshly grated coconut. Serve warm.

Serves 4 to 6   Preparation time: 15 mins   Cooking time: 20 mins

Coconut Cake   Pancong

2 cups (200 g) freshly grated coconut,
  or 1 1/2 cups (120 g) unsweetened
  desiccated coconut moistened with
  3/4 cup (185 ml) warm milk
1/3 cup (50 g) glutinous rice flour
1/3 cup (50 g) rice flour
1/4 cup (50 g) sugar
1/2 teaspoon salt

1 Combine all the ingredients in a mixing bowl and knead for 3 minutes until the dough is smooth and pulls away from the sides of the bowl.
2 Preheat the oven to 350°F (180°C).
3 Dust a cake pan with a little rice flour and press the dough into it with your fingers. Bake in the oven for about 35 minutes until the cake is golden brown and cooked. Remove from the heat and set aside to cool.
4 To remove the cake from the pan, run a knife between the pan and the sides to loosen, then place a platter over the pan and invert it. Slice the cake into serving pieces and serve at room temperature.

Serves 6 to 8   Preparation time: 10 mins   Cooking time: 35 mins

Glutinous Rice Cakes with Palm Sugar   Wajik

There are many variations on this popular cake, which can be stored in the refrigerator for several days. It is normally served at room temperature, but can be served warm topped with coconut cream. Another variation adds diced ripe jackfruit or raisins when the rice is partially cooked.

1 cup (200 g) uncooked glutinous rice
1/2 cup (90 g) shaved palm sugar
1/2 cup (125 ml) water
1 pandanus leaf, tied in a knot,
  or 1 drop pandanus extract
1/4 cup (60 ml) thick coconut milk
Pinch of salt

1 Rinse the glutinous rice in several changes of water until the water runs clear, then soak overnight.
2 Line a steamer basket with a cheesecloth and spread the soaked glutinous rice evenly on the cloth. Steam the rice for 15 minutes, then turn and fluff it up with a fork and steam for 10 more minutes until cooked.
3 In a saucepan, bring the sugar and water to a boil over medium heat and then simmer uncovered, stirring occasionally, until the syrup has reduced to half, about 15 minutes. Add all the other ingredients and mix well. Continue to simmer for 3 to 5 more minutes and remove from the heat.
4 Combine the cooked glutinous rice and coconut milk mixture in a large saucepan and mix well, then cook over low heat, stirring from time to time, until the mixture thickens and becomes sticky, 10 to 15 minutes. Remove from the heat and discard the pandanus leaf, if using.
5 Transfer the cake to a lightly greased shallow cake pan or tray (about 7 in/ 17 cm across), smoothing the surface with the back of a wet spoon, and set aside to cool. Cut the cake into squares or diamond shapes and serve at room temperature.

Note: To speed up the soaking process, pour boiling water over the glutinous rice after rinsing and allow it to stand for 1 hour. Drain, then pour more boiling water over the rice and soak for another 30 minutes.

Serves 6 to 8   Preparation time: 10 mins + overnight soaking
Cooking time: 1 hour 10 mins

Opposite:Coconut Cake (center), Steamed Banana Cakes (left, recipe provided on page 106) and Glutinous Rice Cakes with Palm Sugar (right).

Sweet Coconut Pancakes Dadar

These pancakes, with a sweet coconut filling known as *unti*, are a popular snack food and are sometimes eaten for breakfast.

1 cup (150 g) flour, sifted
2 eggs
2 cups (500 ml) thick coconut milk
$1/_2$ teaspoon salt
2 tablespoons oil

Coconut Filling (*Unti*)
$1/_2$ cup (100 g) palm sugar or dark brown sugar
$1/_4$ cup (60 ml) water
1 cup (100 g) freshly grated coconut
$1/_4$ teaspoon salt
1 pandanus leaf, tied into a knot

1 Make the Coconut Filling by bringing the sugar and water to a boil in a saucepan. Reduce the heat to low and simmer uncovered for about 10 minutes, stirring occasionally, until the sugar is dissolved and the mixture turns syrupy. Add all the other ingredients and cook, stirring constantly, for 10 to 15 minutes, until the mixture dries up. Remove from the heat, discard the pandanus leaf and set aside.
2 To make the pancakes, combine the flour, eggs, coconut milk and salt in a mixing bowl, and whisk into a smooth batter that has a pouring consistency. Strain to remove any lumps. Lightly grease a non-stick wok or skillet and heat over low heat. Stir the batter and ladle 1 scoop (about 3 tablespoons) onto the pan and turn the pan to obtain a thin round layer, about 7 in (18 cm) in diameter. Cook until the pancake sets and begins to brown, then flip it over and cook for a few seconds on the other side, and remove from the heat. Continue to make the pancakes until all the batter is used up.
3 To assemble, place a pancake on a flat surface and top with 2 tablespoons of the Coconut Filling. Fold one side of the pancake over the filling, then fold in the sides and roll up tightly into a cylinder. Assemble the remaining pancakes in the same manner.

Note: The pancakes and Coconut Filling can both be made in advance and refrigerated; allow to warm to room temperature before assembling.

Makes 12 pancakes   Preparation time: 45 mins   Cooking time: 35 mins

Banana Fritters

This is a great way to use up over-ripe bananas, by mashing them up with flour, sugar and coconut cream, and deep-frying them.

2 large or 6 small over-ripe bananas (about 10 oz/300 g), peeled
1 tablespoon sugar
$1/_4$ teaspoon salt (optional)
1 tablespoon flour
$1/_4$ cup (60 ml) coconut cream
Oil, for deep-frying

1 In a mixing bowl, mash the bananas with the sugar, salt (if using), flour and coconut cream into a sticky, slightly moist batter.

2 Heat the oil in a wok or large saucepan until very hot. Using very moist fingers, pinch about 1 heaped tablespoon of the batter, roll it into a ball and gently lower it into the hot oil. Deep-fry for 3 to 5 minutes, turning occasionally, until crispy and golden brown on all sides. Do not overcrowd the pan with the batter or the temperature of the oil will drop. Remove from the hot oil and drain on paper towels.

3 Transfer to a serving platter and serve warm with ice cream or a bit of coconut cream on top.

Serves 4   Preparation time: 10 mins   Cooking time: 15 mins

Steamed Banana Cakes   Kue Nagasari

Bananas are the most widely available fruit throughout Indonesia, so it's not surprising that they feature in many desserts and cakes.

6 small or 2 large ripe bananas
$1^1/_4$ cup (150 g) rice flour
4 tablespoons mung bean flour or tapioca flour
2 cups (500 ml) thin coconut milk
$1/_4$ cup (50 g) sugar
Pinch of salt
Twelve 7-in (18-cm) square pieces of banana leaf, for wrapping
Toothpicks, to fasten

1 Peel and halve each small banana or if using large bananas, slice each diagonally into six $1/_2$-in (1-cm) thick slices. Set aside.

2 Combine both types of flour and $1^1/_2$ cups (325 ml) of the coconut milk in a bowl and mix into a smooth batter, free of any lumps. Set aside.

3 Combine the remaining coconut milk, sugar and salt in a saucepan, and heat over medium heat, mixing well until the sugar is dissolved. Bring to a boil, then pour in the batter and continue to cook, stirring constantly until the mixture thickens, 5 to 10 minutes. Remove from the heat and set aside to cool.

4 Scald the banana leaves by pouring boiling water over them in a basin, so they become flexible. Drain and place the leaves on a clean work surface.

5 To wrap the cakes, spread 2 tablespoons of the flour mixture across the center of a piece of banana leaf. Lay a slice of the banana on top and then spread another 2 tablespoons of the flour mixture over it, covering the banana. Wrap by folding one side of the banana leaf over the filling, then the other, forming a tight parcel. Tuck both ends underneath and fasten with toothpicks. Continue to wrap the remaining ingredients in this manner.

6 Steam the parcels in a wok on a rack over boiling water or in a steamer for about 20 minutes. Remove from the heat and allow to cool before serving.

Note: Mung bean flour (*tepong hoen kwe*) is sold in paper-wrapped cylinders—sometimes, the flour is colored pink or green and the paper wrapper correspondingly colored. It gives a more delicate texture to desserts than rice flour, although the latter is an acceptable substitute.

Makes 12 cakes   Preparation time: 25 mins   Cooking time: 35 mins

Sweet Sago Rolls with Palm Sugar Syrup   Ongol-ongol

An inexpensive dessert in Indonesia where sago flour, palm sugar and coconut are readily available.

1 cup (120 g) sago flour (see note)
   or tapioca flour
1 cup (185 g) shaved palm sugar or
   dark brown sugar
3$^1/_2$ cups (875 ml) water
2 pandanus leaves, tied in a knot,
   or $^1/_4$ teaspoon pandanus extract
Large square of banana leaf or
   parchment paper
Toothpicks, to fasten
1 cup (100 g) freshly grated coconut
   or 1 cup (80 g) lightly moistened
   unsweetened dried coconut flakes
$^1/_2$ teaspoon salt

Palm Sugar Syrup
$^1/_2$ cup (100 g) shaved palm sugar
$^1/_2$ cup (125 ml) water

1 Make the Palm Sugar Syrup by bringing the palm sugar and water to a boil over high heat in a saucepan. Reduce the heat to low, simmer uncovered for about 10 minutes, stirring from time to time, until the sugar is dissolved and the mixture turns syrupy. Remove from the heat and set aside to cool.
2 Combine the sago or tapioca flour, palm sugar and water in a saucepan and mix well. Add the pandanus leaves or extract and bring the mixture to a boil over high heat. Reduce the heat to low and simmer uncovered for about 30 minutes, stirring from time to time until the mixture thickens. Remove from the heat and discard the pandanus leaves if using. Set aside to cool slightly.
3 When cool enough to handle, place the mixture on the piece of banana leaf or parchment paper and roll it up to form a compact cylinder. Fasten the ends of the roll with toothpicks and set aside to cool completely.
4 Combine the grated coconut and salt, and mix well.
5 To serve, slice the rolls into disks, sprinkled with a little grated coconut (mixed with salt) and drizzle the Palm Sugar Syrup over it.

Note: Sago flour, made from the grated trunk of the sago palm tree is produced in many Indonesian and Pacific islands. It is sold in powder form in plastic packets in Asian supermarkets, as is tapioca flour (also known as cassava flour).

Serves 6 to 8   Preparation time: 20 mins   Cooking time: 45 mins

Sweet Rice Flour Porridge   Bubur Sumsum

Various types of flour made from sago, tapioca, rice and small, round green mung beans are widely used for making simple desserts and cakes. Bubur Sumsum is the Indonesian equivalent of a Jewish mother's Chicken Soup—if you have a problem, eat a bowl of Bubur Sumsum and all will be well.

1$^1/_2$ cups (180 g) rice flour
6 cups (1$^1/_2$ liters) water
$^1/_2$ cup (50 g) freshly grated coconut
   or $^1/_2$ cup (40 g) lightly moistened
   unsweetened dried coconut flakes
$^1/_2$ teaspoon salt
1 portion Palm Sugar Syrup (see
   above)

1 Make the Palm Sugar Syrup by following the above recipe (step 1).
2 Combine the flour and water in a mixing bowl and mix well. Strain the mixture through a fine sieve to remove any lumps. Place in a non-stick saucepan and bring the mixture to a boil over high heat, then reduce the heat and simmer uncovered for about 30 minutes, stirring from time to time until it thickens. Remove from the heat and allow to cool.
3 Combine the grated coconut and salt, and mix well.
4 To serve, spoon the rice flour porridge into individual serving bowls and top with a little grated coconut (mixed with the salt), followed by a drizzling of Palm Sugar Syrup over it.

Serves 4 to 6   Preparation time: 10 mins   Cooking time: 30 mins